Meeting New Challenges in the Foreign Language Classroom

CENTRAL STATES CONFERENCE ON THE TEACHING OF FOREIGN LANGUAGES

Officers and Directors, 1993–94 (followed by year term ends)

Meeting New Challenges in the Foreign Language Classroom

Selected Papers from the 1994
Central States Conference

Edited by

Gale K. Crouse
University of Wisconsin–Eau Claire

Coeditors

Patrick T. Raven
School District of Waukesha, Wisconsin

Marcia H. Rosenbusch
Iowa State University, Ames, Iowa

National Textbook Company
NTC a division of NTC *Publishing Group* • Lincolnwood, Illinois USA

Published by National Textbook Company, a division of NTC Publishing Group.
© 1994 by NTC Publishing Group, 4255 West Touhy Avenue,
Lincolnwood (Chicago), Illinois 60646-1975 U.S.A.
Manufactured in the United States of America.

4 5 6 7 8 9 0 VP 9 8 7 6 5 4 3 2 1

Preface

The desire for educational reform is prompting many approaches to altering the educational system from kindergarten through the university. The current movement for change is forcing all foreign language professionals to seek new solutions to both old and new challenges. They are being asked to provide different methods of instruction, to create different approaches to assessment, to incorporate an increasing amount of technology, and to restructure the academic year and day.

The theme "Challenges for a New Era" provided the organizational layout for the 1994 Central States Conference held in Kansas City, Missouri, in partnership with the Foreign Language Association of Missouri (FLAM). Some of the topics addressed in the 28 workshops and 136 sessions at the 26th annual conference were new approaches to assessment, redesigned courses, restructured curriculum, growth in elementary programs, new technology, and professional development. Also among the sessions were three focus sessions dealing with community college programs, middle school programs, and the development of national standards for foreign languages. The keynote speaker, Dr. Frederic Jones, focused on the daily challenge of the classroom in his address, "Positive Classroom Management: Where Discipline Meets Instruction." The luncheon speaker, Dr. Robert Lafayette, considered the content of instruction.

The strength of the Central States Conference is the dedication of the foreign language educators who come together annually to celebrate triumphs, to explore new approaches, and to seek solutions to the many challenges we face in the foreign language classroom.

Mary M. Carr
1994 Program Chair

Dedication

This volume is dedicated to the memory of Lorraine A. Strasheim. Lorraine, a founder of the Central States Conference on the Teaching of Foreign Languages, published frequently in the Central States Conference *Report* and edited the 1991 volume. It is most appropriate that the present volume be dedicated to her, for Lorraine was a strong supporter of publications such as this, which, in her words, "are usable" by classroom teachers, helping them enrich the learning experiences of their students.

Lorraine was an inspiration to foreign language teachers through her perceptive insights and her understanding of what we as foreign language educators try to convey to our students—the ability and skills necessary to live peaceably in a world of diverse languages and cultures. She was a great communicator, not only in writing, but from the podium, always in demand to present at conferences and filling meeting rooms to overflowing.

Her many ideas have become an important part of the professional literature in foreign language education. Her contributions range from such titles as "The Issue: Multi-Level Classes" to "Winding Down the Year Positively, Painlessly, and Pleasurably." Although she had a vast knowledge and understanding of the theoretical basis for second language acquisition, she always concentrated on issues that affected the classroom teacher directly. For Lorraine, teaching and teacher education were goal driven—driven by the desire to help students attain competencies that were clearly defined and tangibly observable and would allow students, teachers, and parents to realize that one learned language in order to understand various ways of daily life through the language. And she went beyond foreign language education into social studies and curriculum development in general. Her work in developing integrated curricular materials for social studies and foreign language teachers was recognized by the American Forum for Global Education by awarding her posthumously the Global Apple Award during the Forum's 1993 conference in Indianapolis.

It is in the spirit of the "Friendly Conference" that we recognize one of our own whom we miss and memorialize through the publication of this volume.

—Walter H. Bartz
Martha Nyikos

Contents

Encountering Other Cultures

Measuring Proficiency

Serving the Wider Community

Introduction:
Meeting New Challenges in the Foreign Language Classroom

Gale K. Crouse
University of Wisconsin–Eau Claire

The title of this volume, *Meeting New Challenges in the Foreign Language Classroom,* is an echo of the 1994 Central States Conference theme, "Challenges for a New Era." For foreign language teachers, the terms *challenges* and *opportunities* are more than politically correct euphemisms of the 1990s. Our profession today stands at a crossroads. The highly successful oral proficiency initiative of the 1980s has led to a need to implement proficiency guidelines in the other skills areas, a project that is already well under way. A recent movement to define national standards has brought us to a point barely imaginable a decade ago—inclusion in a nationwide core curriculum. Ray Clifford, 1993 ACTFL president, has written that "the greatest advantage of this formal recognition of foreign languages at the national policy level is not what it will do for us, but what it will allow us to do" (1993). This is our day of opportunity!

In this twenty-second volume in the Central States Conference *Report* series, ten articles address some of the challenges for foreign language teachers today. Authors point to areas that merit our attention as we prepare our world to enter a new millennium.

Defining the Profession

In a lead article, June Phillips and Jamie Draper discuss national education reform and the development of performance standards in the field of foreign languages. They succinctly summarize where we have been and point to changes we face for the future as the profession continues to move forward.

Addressing Diversity

One particular challenge to foreign language teachers is to deliver the discipline to a wider audience than has traditionally been the case. Charles

Hancock shows that African-Americans are notably underrepresented in foreign language enrollments and suggests that a better understanding of Afro-American culture will allow teachers to reach these students more effectively.

Audrey Heining-Boynton studies the at-risk student, discussing the various characteristics of these students and exploring the involvement, potential and real, of foreign language teachers. She concludes that foreign languages can no longer be considered the sole domain of the traditional college-bound student but must be open to accommodate the needs of the entire student population.

Re-Viewing the Curriculum

As we adapt to a more diverse clientele, an effective and efficient curriculum must remain our goal. Robert Davis and Jay Siskin consider the advanced conversation class, note the frustrations it often causes both teachers and students, and propose a method to "get them to talk" through task content and sequencing.

Teacher education is the focus of the article by Flore Zéphir, who believes that teachers have a profound impact on shaping society. Because only those who are truly "culturally competent" will be prepared for tomorrow's classroom, this author stresses that multiculturalism and sociolinguistics must become an integral part of teacher-education programs.

Encountering Other Cultures

An ongoing and ever-expanding challenge to teachers is the effective communication of cultural concepts. Gerhard Fischer considers how modern communications technology, notably electronic mail, can facilitate intercultural learning through direct communication with people in other cultures. He describes one such project, noting how easily a desire to communicate can also result in miscommunication.

Jayne Abrate reports on a very successful experience in using the Minitel to communicate cultural information. By pairing French and U.S. classes in a "correspondance scolaire," teachers guided students to a greater understanding of and appreciation for attitudes and practices of another culture. The author proposes other projects for bringing students together via Minitel.

Measuring Proficiency

Donna Clementi and Paul Sandrock explore the challenge of meaningful assessment in the proficiency-oriented classroom. Their hypothesis is a simple one: if we teach for proficiency, then we must also test for proficiency. They make valuable suggestions for designing assessments that do indeed measure proficiency goals.

One form of assessment that is receiving more and more attention today is the portfolio. Aleidine Moeller presents a thorough study of portfolio assessment and applies it specifically to measuring competence in foreign languages. Language learning, she believes, must emphasize process; portfolio assessment offers the teacher an opportunity to measure growth over time in all skill areas.

Serving the Wider Community

Richard Kalfus considers the role of the community college in foreign language education. New recommendations that stress proficiency objectives have been issued by the American Association of Community Colleges. This article contains a report of those recommendations and describes projects that are now under way to meet goals set for foreign language instruction in the community college.

The volume closes with an annotated bibliography of readings suggested by the authors and editors. While the reading list is far from complete, it will serve to guide readers to more information as together we accept these "Challenges for a New Era."

Reference

Clifford, Ray T. 1993. "Message from the President." *Foreign Language Annals* 26,3: 399.

Acknowledgments

The selection of articles for a volume such as this is not an easy undertaking; there are simply too many good papers for the space available. Each manuscript submitted was read and evaluated by at least five individuals—the editor, the two coeditors, and at least two other foreign language professionals. The thoughtful comments and lucid suggestions they offered made the final selection and editing a much easier task. The following individuals deserve profound thanks for willingly contributing their time and energy to this project: Leon Book, Southeast Missouri State University, Cape Girardeau; Lynn Haire, Ferndale Public Schools, Plymouth, Michigan; Linda Hertzler-Crumm, Iowa State University, Ames; Nancy Humbach, Miami University, Oxford, Ohio; John Katzenmeyer, Zion-Benton Township High School, Zion, Illinois; Mike McKinnon, Janesville School District, Janesville, Wisconsin; Emily Spinelli, University of Michigan–Dearborn; Toni Theisen,

Thompson/Loveland Schools, Fort Collins, Colorado; Nile Vernon, University of Northern Iowa, Cedar Falls; Karen Weiss, Bayview High School, Milwaukee, Wisconsin; Patricia Westphal, Central College, Pella, Iowa; Patricia Davis-Wiley, University of Tennessee, Knoxville; JoAnne Wilson, Glen Arbor, Michigan.

Special recognition is due to the two coeditors, Patrick Raven, School District of Waukesha, Wisconsin, and Marcia Rosenbusch, Iowa State University, Ames, whose loyal assistance, sound advice, and gentle reminders made the work proceed smoothly and on schedule. Finally, thanks could not be complete without mention of the NTC team of Keith Fry and Geof Garvey who were ever patient, understanding, and professionally alert.

1
National Standards and Assessments:
What Does It Mean for the Study of Second Languages in the Schools?[1]

June K. Phillips
Weber State University

Jamie B. Draper
American Council on the Teaching of Foreign Languages

There is absolutely no doubt that the political and educational agendas in our country are reverberating with the dynamic of change and the desire for reform. It is equally certain that change drives the professional lives of second language educators as well. Professional changes have confronted us for a number of years now as we struggle with a paradigm shift that has challenged us to revise our thinking about the goals and objectives of language instruction. Broader purposes for language study and a growing research base in second language acquisition have led to instructional approaches that emphasize the developmental aspect of language learning rather than a mastery model; envisioning the student as an interactive and creative learner has enabled us to provide richer content through authentic documents and to allow a more process-centered approach within the expressive modalities.

Even as second language teachers strive to translate more fully communicative approaches into classroom instruction, along comes educational reform with its emphasis on content standards and new assessments. In Washington and in state capitals, two questions dominate the discussion of education:

- What should students *know* and be able to *do?*
- How good is good enough?

The search for answers to these questions has resulted in a governmental focus on the creation of content standards (knowing and doing) and performance standards (how good) in a number of academic disciplines. At the beginning, the very real fear existed that foreign languages would be ignored in the process. Fear of being left out has shifted to the challenge of being included.

"Good Fortune Comes to Those Who Are Prepared"

Right now, everywhere one turns foreign languages are gaining recognition. The "core curriculum" as recently redefined by the National Education Goals Panel includes foreign languages; the National Assessment of Educational Progress (NAEP) has slated work to begin on measurement design for foreign languages in a few years; a national standards project for foreign languages has been funded by the U.S. Department of Education. None of this has come about by accident. As ACTFL's 1993 president, Ray Clifford, stated in a message to the membership, "Good things come to those who are prepared."

In late 1989, then-President George Bush invited the members of the National Governors' Association, headed by then-Governor Bill Clinton, to a historic education summit in Charlottesville, Virginia. At that gathering, the six National Education Goals were hammered out. They were notable to us for their exclusion of foreign languages as a critical subject area, yet the announced intention of this goal-setting process was to make U.S. schools the "best in the world." When a series of public hearings on the goals was announced in 1990, coincidentally less than a week before the annual meeting of the Joint National Committee for Languages (JNCL), the foreign language profession was prepared. Delegations to the hearings were quickly organized, and foreign language educators testified at each regional forum. At the conclusion of the hearings, the National Educational Goals Panel acknowledged that foreign languages were an important part of the school curriculum.

As the national standards movement gathered steam in 1991, the Council for Basic Education released its now infamous "Wall Chart," once again noted for its exclusion of foreign languages. ACTFL responded to this challenge by drafting a series of outcome statements for three sequences of instruction. This draft document, based upon work done over the last ten years with *Proficiency Guidelines* (ACTFL 1986), received generally positive reaction from the field. While that document was narrowly targeted at proficiency-oriented outcomes and not broadly enough based for actual school standards, it did demonstrate that the foreign language profession was ready to move forward in the standards arena.

In the fall of 1992, as ACTFL and the three largest language-specific organizations in the nation, the American Association of Teachers of French (AATF), the American Association of Teachers of German (AATG), and the American Association of Teachers of Spanish and Portuguese (AATSP), were gathering to discuss a collaborative effort to coordinate professionwide teacher-education standards, it was learned that the U.S. Department of Education would be interested in reviewing a proposal to develop national standards in foreign language education. The meeting already in progress quickly turned into a planning session for such an undertaking; three weeks later, a proposal was submitted to the Department of Education.

A decade of work in developing consensus in the field and in building political awareness had paid off. The foreign language profession stands ready to face the challenges of participating as a full partner in national education reform efforts.

Foreign Language Standards among Other Standards Projects

The various standards initiatives, complex in themselves, become more so as a result of the number of projects being developed simultaneously. Making sense out of these initiatives is no easy task. Standards are being developed for grade levels, such as middle school; delivery standards are being drafted for the schools; national teacher certification standards are under way; finally, content and performance standards projects in the various disciplines have been funded. Questions surround all these concerning compatibility (fit among the standards), feasibility (fit in the school day), and accountability (fit with measurement and evaluation).

It must be recognized that when the foreign language profession was presented with the opportunity to develop disciplinary standards for K–12, the decision to accept the challenge was taken with both hesitation and enthusiasm. Hesitation because the field was in flux. State curricular frameworks certainly illustrated the impact of a proficiency orientation and communicative goals. Higher education was more mixed and still finds itself in the throes of debating goals, approaches, and even rationale for foreign language study. Enthusiasm because this opportunity to be in the core curriculum will not knock again if the door remains closed. Therefore, ACTFL, AATF, AATG, and AATSP decided to accept the challenge to draft standards that meet the government's criteria of "world class" and for "all students." The bottom line was: "It will be done. If we don't do it, who will?"

All the disciplinary standards projects, including ours, confront certain tensions as a result of this national initiative. The impetus for the Goals 2000 document (now titled *Educate America 2000* in the legislation) arose from the rhetoric of global competitiveness. As U.S. students suffered in numerous academic and environmental comparisons with students from other highly developed countries, dissatisfaction with the schools grew. The setting of standards that are "world class" was seen as a way of improving academics here. The paradox is, however, that the U.S. fears and abhors a national curriculum; the very words are anathema to the U.S. public. Yet every country with which we seek to compete bases its educational system on a national curriculum.

Other tensions abound as well: There is tension between disciplinary and delivery standards. Disciplinary standards have the potential to discriminate against youngsters in inadequate schools unless "opportunity to learn" monies are available. Delivery standards tend to be based upon the appearance of what a school has, not what it mandates for learning. In our case, the fact that foreign languages have never been solidly placed in the curriculum below the high school level has also meant that we have only recently begun to address teacher preparation specifically for the younger student.

Another point of tension: While the standards will be voluntary (to get around the question of a national curriculum), federal funding may be tied to efforts to implement the standards. There is tension between top-down standards, i.e., from bureaucrats and experts, with bottom-up standards, i.e., grass-roots efforts in schools. All projects grapple with these tensions plus others that are rooted in the discipline.

A few of the issues with which the foreign language task force wrestles: Among the disciplines, we alone are not already safely ensconced in a K–12 sequence. Do we therefore write standards as though foreign language is really K–12? Or how do we write standards for sequences that have a variety of entry points? Other standards projects target assessments for grades 4, 8, and 12 because the National Assessment of Educational Progress had designated those areas. Our student enrollments peak in grades 9 and 10. New ground must also be plowed in foreign language education because of the way standards projects have defined content and performance standards. The changes that have dominated our profession for the last decade have concentrated upon performance. In the past (sometimes in the present) we defined content as linguistic and taught the forms of language, the phonology, the morphology, the syntactical rules, and the lexicon in the expectation that learners would be able to express meaning. The proficiency orientation focused us on outcomes, competencies, tasks, functions, i.e., performance. It may be worth noting that other disciplines take pride and comfort at delineating the content that students should know and are venturing into the unknown as they attempt to describe performances. At the opposite end, we must go beyond proficiency and redefine the knowledge base upon which our discipline is built. That brings out another tension: *describing* content without *prescribing* it for state and local purposes.

What the Field Believes about National Standards in Foreign Language Education

The task force gathered input from the field at the outset and it will continue to do so.[2] During the summer and fall of 1993, the standards project, with the assistance of regional and state leaders, distributed a questionnaire to more than 30,000 foreign language teachers across the country asking for their input on a variety of issues that must be addressed prior to any standard setting. The responses were reassuring both in quantity, providing necessary evidence of dissemination, and in quality of response.

As expected, there was a great deal of consensus surrounding major issues such as whether *all* students should learn a foreign language (response: yes), and when foreign language study should begin (response: as early as possible). In other areas there was less consensus and less understanding of the framing of the question.

The survey attested to a tremendous need to develop a strong rationale for foreign language programs. Although the profession overwhelmingly supports foreign language study by all students, it is unable to provide anything other than a few catch phrases (e.g., international competitiveness, national security) as arguments to sustain that position. Given the tenuous status of many foreign language programs in the country, this issue demands immediate attention.

It was somewhat surprising to note that, while the profession endorses an early start to language instruction, it does not necessarily advocate a long sequence of study. Many of the same people who wanted language instruction to begin in kindergarten responded "four years" to the question, "What should the minimum sequence be?" On a different note, several respondents felt that the focus should not be on years of instruction but on outcomes and on uninterrupted sequences. In other words, it should not matter how long students pursue foreign language study as long as they develop an appropriate (but undefined) level of proficiency.

Another major issue concerns the levels at which standards should be targeted. Should they be developed according to grade level (4, 5, 6, . . .), by cluster of grades (elementary, middle school, etc.), or by stage of language development? The responses to the questionnaire indicated that combining a measure of stage of language development with either grade level or clusters of grades might be the best avenue. The major concern seemed to be that the standards be developed in such a way as to allow for maximum flexibility at the local level for achieving them. No small task!

On the issue of what content to include in addition to skills, the dominant response was culture, including the history, geography, politics, arts, and traditions of the target-language cultures. Frequently mentioned were cultural understandings and learning to recognize that there are many different ways of doing things. Many respondents also suggested content-based instruction and interdisciplinary studies. A surprising number of people, however, thought that the standards should focus exclusively on skills and that other content should be left to the individual teachers, if dealt with at all.

Finally, though this initial survey showed a great deal of consensus, it also indicated a lack of information about national education issues as evidenced by responses to questions regarding the National Assessment of Educational Progress and in the standards development process in general. This clearly signals to those involved in the standards process and in leadership roles in professional organizations that we must be diligent in informing the profession not only about the progress of the project but likewise about the impact of national education reform efforts and directions.

Toward New Assessments

The relief in the standards-drafting project for foreign language educators lies in our recent and continuing experience with performance assessments. The Oral Proficiency Interview for speaking and subsequent classroom adaptations have given us a tool for evaluating the skill we and students had long sought but had rarely measured. Many in our field have borrowed from our language arts colleagues by experimenting with writing as process, reading as an interactive process, even utilizing a holistic approach to language learning. We have used journal writing and letter and E-mail correspondence to provide students with an audience other than "teacher" for their written expression. Authentic documents rich in meaning form the basis of instruction in the receptive skills. Research into the comprehension processes, the power of metacognitive and strategy training for learners, and our increasing confidence in exploiting the learner's background knowledge have led to whole new approaches to reading and listening, approaches not dissimilar to those of whole language. We are positioned well to incorporate the new global assessments into our discipline because they parallel newer instructional approaches.

In virtually every area of new assessments, some of which are being mandated by states, foreign language teachers have been receptive. For example, both models of portfolios work well for us, the "best work" and "progress" types. The idea of student performances—whether in interviews, in problem-solving scenarios, or in summaries or protocols of information understood from video or magazines—fits well with a communicative orientation. In sum, our profession should do well by new assessments that prove to our students, their parents, and the community how effectively language can be used.

Teachers as Agents of Change

The reality is that the changes we are facing will be major for some teachers and programs, minor for others. An important dimension of all standards projects resides in the provision for professional development. Teachers must not become targets of reform but must assume the role of agents of reform. For us, the challenge lies in managing change with a minimum of discomfort, without chaos, but realistically one must be ready to tolerate a bit of ambiguity, take a few risks, think divergently—in essence think just as critically in our roles as teachers as we would want students to do in their roles as learners.

At this juncture in our profession, instructional change requires a totally new dimension of professional development as well as a revamping of teacher-education programs. The day of "methods" and prescriptions and "cookbooks" of neat ideas has passed. When dealing with the spectrum of human communication, it no longer suffices to exert tight instructional control that carefully dispenses prescribed structures and vocabulary and formulaic messages. Learners must also be prepared to confront unique utterances and text. They must become adept at processes and not just products. The bottom line is *empowerment*. To empower learners, we must first have empowered teachers: teachers empowered to reflect on their classes, teachers empowered to observe learning and facilitate it, teachers empowered with strong proficiencies in the target languages so that they feel confident in using materials from a variety of sources and content areas. We wanted to be decision makers; we now have the opportunity to be so; we also need the information upon which to base wise decisions. Inservice and preservice programs must prepare us to *think* and not to imitate sheepishly or follow strict formulas. Most important, as teachers we must decide what to change, when to change, and how to change so that the result is not chaos and we are only slightly discomforted as we abandon fruitless practices and substitute more potent ones.

The national standards project could succeed in changing how children and young adults learn second languages in this nation; to do so, the profession must agree to move forward with instruction and assessment that recognizes the value of foreign language study for a broad spectrum of learners. Teachers, too, will have to embrace the concept of lifelong learning for themselves so that they continue to expand their linguistic proficiencies, their knowledge of the cultures for which they hope students develop understandings, and the research base upon which viable instructional approaches are built.

Notes

1. A portion of this article is taken from a keynote address, "National Standards, Global Assessments: Galactic or Microcosmic Change?" prepared by June K. Phillips for the Pennsylvania State Modern Language Association in October 1993.
2. The task force charged with drafting the standards is chaired by Christine Brown (Glastonbury Public Schools, CT). Members of the task force are Martha Abbott (Fairfax County Public Schools, VA), Keith Cothrun (Las Cruces High School, NM), Beverly Harris-Schenz (University of Pittsburgh), Denise B. Mesa (Dade County Public Schools, FL), Genelle Morain (The University of Georgia), Marjorie Tussing (California State University at Fullerton), Guadalupe Valdés (Stanford University), John Webb (Hunter College High School, NY), and Thomas E. Welch (Kentucky Department of Education).

Reference

American Council on the Teaching of Foreign Languages. 1986. *Proficiency Guidelines*. Yonkers, NY: ACTFL.

2
Cultural Roots and Academic Achievement:
Is There a Problem in Foreign Language Study?

Charles R. Hancock
The Ohio State University

> Begin where you are, but don't stay there.
> *(Zambian proverb)*

In the 1980s and 1990s, an unfortunate and alarming trend continues in foreign language study: African-American students enroll in and continue their foreign language study in very small numbers when compared to students from other cultural groups. Moreover, African-American students tend not to achieve as well as other students, even when they do enroll in such study. These claims refer to the general populace of African-American students and recognize, of course, that exceptions occur.

Statements such as these demand evidence. Unfortunately, statistics that show the number of African-American students in various foreign language classes and their achievement levels are virtually impossible to gather. One reason is that, except in certain limited cases, federal and state laws of privacy prohibit the asking of one's ethnic origin or the collection of data and its analysis by race or ethnic origin.

Descriptive statistics are only one database, however. Every language teacher can "collect" data (and probably has done so) by simply observing the presence or absence of African-American students over the years in foreign language classes, especially advanced classes. Additionally, any language teacher can speak to the achievement level of his or her students, including African-American students, despite the lack of a set of statistics.

It is this "informal teacher database" that the reader is asked to consider here, since these teacher perspectives are often as accurate as any developed by researchers. For purposes of the discussion, the reader is asked to forego statistical evidence and accept the assumption that there is a problem with both enrollment and level of achievement of African-American students in foreign language study in the United States.[1]

Two additional assumptions form key bases of this article. First, while much of the focus here is on African-American students, the intent is not to ignore other ethnic minority groups, such as Asians, Hispanics, or Europeans. Rather, those of us who have had the good fortune to learn about our own cultures must serve as advocates for doing so whenever the opportunity arises. Our own cultures should not be advocated at the expense of other cultures or groups, however.

Another assumption is that only some aspects of achievement are measured by standardized paper-and-pencil (or computerized) tests. Those who set policies and determine how achievement is measured define reality in terms that are advantageous to their own purposes. One should not be misled into thinking that academic achievement is "objective" and can always be measured best through tests such as the SAT, ACT, NTE, GRE, CEEB, or other national educational assessment projects. Such testing typically measures only part of what students have achieved.

Nobles has defined culture as "a human process representing the vast structure of behaviors, ideas, attitudes, values, habits, beliefs, customs, language, rituals, ceremonies and practices peculiar to a particular group of people and which provides them with a general design for living and patterns for interpreting reality" (Nobles 1990: 23). It is the final part of this definition that should be especially noted here. The ways that African-American students behave in classrooms may indeed be based on an Afro-centric "design for living and patterns for interpreting reality."

There have been notable successes in teaching for achievement in minority cultures. Jaime Escalante, in the Escuela Secundaria Garfield in East Los Angeles, experienced tremendous success in teaching mathematics to high-risk students whom others had given up on. His work is now widely recognized and was the basis for the film *Stand and Deliver*. The essence of what made the students at Garfield learn and which is showing up in the students in another school where he worked, Hiram Johnson High School in Sacramento, is what Escalante calls *ganas,* or "strong desire." Escalante's students, often inner-city Hispanic youth, demonstrated a strong desire to succeed and an ability to sacrifice; Escalante was able to reach these students through his keen understanding of and ability to teach to their cultural backgrounds. As he recently stated, "En el futuro, espero ver a un número cada vez mayor de Hispanos en la cúspide de los campos de la matemática y la ciencia, que ayuden a nuestro país a continuar siendo fuerte" [In the future, I hope to see more and more Hispanics at the top of the math and science fields, helping our country stay strong] (Escalante 1992: 23).

Marva Collins (Collins and Tamarkin 1982) has also shown tremendous success in her efforts on behalf of black youngsters in Chicago. Her success is based on setting high expectations for her students, helping students spend a lot of time on task, and using active teaching behaviors. Her classroom includes heavy emphasis on cooperation, flexibility, collective responsibility, autonomy, and strong adult leadership, traits traditionally found in many African-American family settings. The classroom in which Collins works is also characterized by her use of patterns commonly found in African-American churches. She uses a great deal of choral and responsive reading and audience participation and identifies a moral or personal message in passages read.

Escalante (1992), Collins and Tamarkin (1982), Brice-Heath (1989), and Haskins (1992) have all reported ways to bridge the gap between home and school by engaging students in culturally relevant learning. The hypothesis advocated in this article is that by engaging in culturally relevant learning for youngsters, we can, in fact, improve the students' academic performance.

Villegas (1991) documents the position that "teachers can have a positive impact on the academic growth of minority students." She believes that "Good teachers must be sensitive to the cultural characteristics of the learners and have the skills needed to accommodate these characteristics in the classroom" (p. iii). The fact is, of course, that while people may give lip service to this perspective, many teachers of African-Americans in the United States are white, middle-class individuals who have had very little contact with people of color or, in many cases, who may be culturally very different from them. As professionals, we are always trying to grow, sharpen our perspectives, and make a more profound difference in the lives of our students and colleagues.[2] We can be sensitive in the ways that Villegas means, however, only if we know what the issues are and deal with them within our own professional environment.

In a moving and important article entitled "Race and the Schooling of Black Americans," Steele (1992) points to some alarming figures on African-Americans and the U.S. educational system.

- 70 percent of all African-American students who enroll in a four-year college drop out at some point, as compared with 40 percent of whites.

- For both blacks and whites the level of preparation, as measured by Scholastic Aptitude Test scores, does not make much difference in who flunks out and who succeeds in college and university studies.

- Even at the highest levels of preparation (combined SAT scores of 1400 and above) in this study only 2 percent to 11 percent of whites flunked out, whereas 8 percent to 33 percent of the blacks did so.

These figures reflect what Steele calls "the rule, not the exception," in his assertion that "From elementary school to graduate school, something depresses black achievement at every level of preparation, even the highest" (p. 70). He goes on to state, "Clearly, something is missing from our understanding of black underachievement" (p. 72). African-American students seem to have a fear, from first grade through graduate school, that in the eyes of those around them their full humanity could fall with a poor answer or a mistaken stroke of a pen.

If Steele is correct, stigma is the culprit that undermines African-American student achievement as effectively as the proverbial lock on the schoolhouse door. In other words, U.S. society stigmatizes people of color and devalues them. One is reminded of the saying that was once popular, "If you're white, you're right; if you're yellow, you're mellow; if you're brown, stick around; if you're black, step back." Rightly or wrongly, sayings like these exist and too often represent a perception of reality that we do not like to acknowledge. Messages like these are still communicated to students, even in subtle ways. For example, it can be seen in studies that show that throughout high school African-American students are twice as likely as white students to receive corporal punishment, to be suspended from school, or to be labeled mentally retarded (Clark 1983; Collison 1987; Steele 1992).

Perhaps the most comprehensive study of the impact of culture on the achievement of African-American youngsters was the publication of Hale-Benson (1988). The author argues convincingly that "Black people participate in a coherent culture that shapes their cognitive development and affects the way they approach academic tasks and the way they behave in academic settings" (p. 21). In this sense, her perspective is similar to Steele's cited above, i.e., that African-American students must operate in an atmosphere that sometimes *feels hostile* to their ways of doing things, and *they often develop defensive reactions that interfere with intellectual performance*. Of course, it should be acknowledged that the sort of *anomie* or intense uneasiness faced by African-Americans is also experienced by other groups in our U.S. society, Native Americans and Hispanics in particular. None of these ethnic groups is typically listed on most charts and graphs as being at the top of the achievement ladder in U.S. schools. In fact, statistics show that, on the whole, these three groups are very often last in terms of standardized measures of achievement. Again, one must quickly add that there are many exceptions within the student populations in these groups.

Hale-Benson (1988) refers to the work of Stodolsky and Lesser that suggests that ethnic groups differ in their patterns of behavior no matter what the social class level is within the ethnic group. Stodolsky and Lesser studied African-American, Puerto Rican, Chinese, and Jewish children, focusing on four mental operations: verbal abilities, reasoning, number facility, and space conceptualization. Their study revealed distinctive differences among the ethnic groups, with the frequency of usage for the various ethnic groups as follows, from highest to lowest:

African-Americans: verbal ability > reasoning > space conceptualization > number ability

Chinese: space conceptualization > number ability > reasoning > verbal ability

Jewish: verbal ability > number ability > reasoning > space conceptualization

Puerto Rican: space conceptualization > number ability > reasoning > verbal ability

One can readily see the relative position of the various operations based on the learner's ethnicity. Verbal ability, for example, is first for African-American and Jewish learners but last for Chinese and Puerto Rican learners, an observation that should be taken into account by teachers of these groups in all disciplines, including foreign languages. Because many of us may have a natural tendency to be suspicious of such generalized studies, however, further research on these topics is still needed.

As classroom teachers, many of us prefer to think that our students are all basically the same. How many of us have said, maybe even publicly, "I treat all my students the same. I try not to look at a student's color"? Some research is beginning to point out that although social class has seemed to be a key variable in academic achievement, ethnicity is emerging as the primary factor. Further research is needed to investigate questions such as the following:

1. To what extent are mental operation patterns predictors of school achievement? Are different patterns associated with school success and success in nonschool contexts?

2. How stable are identified mental operation patterns over time? What role does the school play in modifying distinctive ethnic-group patterns, if indeed they are shown to be detrimental to a group of students' academic success as measured in standard ways?

3. How should students' mental operation patterns be matched to the school's practices and vice-versa?

Clearly, the answers to questions such as these are likely to shape what happens in schools, colleges, and universities in foreign language study as well as in other disciplines.

In an attempt to propose possible solutions to an ongoing problem, some people are suggesting alternative perspectives and initiatives. Akbar (1985) has suggested a description of African-American youngsters based on their African heritage and their U.S. environment. He characterizes the African-American youngster in the following profile:

The African-American Youngster

Is highly affective

Uses language requiring a wide use of many coined interjections

Expresses herself or himself through considerable body language

Relies on words that depend on context for meaning and that have little meaning in themselves

Prefers using expressions that have particular connotations

Adopts a systematic use of nuances of intonation and body language, such as eye movement and positioning

Prefers oral-aural modalities for learning communication

Is highly sensitive to others' nonverbal cues

Seeks to be people oriented

Is sociocentric

Uses internal cues for problem solving

Feels highly empathetic

Likes spontaneity

Adapts rapidly to novel stimuli

Akbar's profile should be considered as a possible part of the solution to raising African-American student achievement because it may help us understand better the cultural patterns and learning styles of African-American students. We owe it to our students to examine avenues that have the potential of stemming the tide of low African-American student achievement, particularly in our field of study, foreign languages, where the numbers of African-American students who choose to continue their foreign language study beyond the beginning required years is abysmally small.

Hilliard (1990) has characterized the question of how to educate African-American children as a "discovery problem" rather than a delivery problem. There is a significant African world view, a set of values and language that continue to shape African-American students, even in ways that they, themselves, may not understand. If we examine the items on Akbar's list and correlate them with Hilliard's notion, we see that many of them relate to communication generally and, more specifically, to language.

Still another promising approach is that of Treisman and his colleagues, first at the University of California at Berkeley and more recently at the University of Texas at Austin. Treisman's research shows that mathematics and science courses have "all too often been the burial grounds for the aspirations of minority students who enter college with the goal of majoring in engineering, or one of the sciences" (Karelis 1993: 67). During his eighteen-month ethnographic study, Treisman found there was a pattern of social and intellectual isolation among the college minority students in his study that eventually led to students' "demoralization, disorientation, and ultimately, their decision to leave the sciences. Many of these students, moreover, dropped out of the University." Might the same patterns not apply to foreign language students? Karelis goes on to describe an important contrast between African-American and Chinese students:

> Many African-American students Treisman observed studied alone and maintained a rigid separation of their academic and social lives. This pattern was in marked contrast to that of Chinese students in Treisman's study, who typically created an academically-focused social group that served to support their aspirations for high achievement. In their informal groups, Chinese students discussed their academic work as well as such topics as interacting with the faculty, the intricacies of getting a needed answer from an administrative office, financial aid, and so on. Treisman believed that creating a rich mathematical environment in which such collaboration was natural, African-American and Hispanic students would be drawn to mathematics and would thrive. (Karelis 1993: 67–68)

The results of Treisman's work are now legendary, and projects based on his work are being widely implemented.[3] According to evaluations of its first seven years, the Treisman project had a "dramatic effect" on both mathematics performance and persistence rates of minority students at Berkeley. Similar results are now being shown in Treisman-type projects at Rutgers University, City College of New York, California Polytechnic State University at San Luis Obispo, and the University of California at San Francisco School of Medicine (Karelis 1993). Clearly, it is possible to change a negative situation into a positive one using cultural roots as a basis for improved academic achievement. It has been done in mathematics, so why not in foreign languages?

Comparisons between U.S. Student Achievement and That of Japanese and Chinese Youngsters in Math and Reading

Approaching the topic from a different perspective from what has been presented so far, one might look at cultural roots and academic achievement from a cross-national perspective. Stevenson and Stigler (1992) conducted two studies, one in 1980 and one in 1987, both of which focused on children's achievement in the United States as compared with that of children in China and Japan. They limited the areas of achievement examined to mathematics and reading, essentially using first- and fifth-grade pupils in several cities. They cite a 1989 report of the National Research Council:

Average students in other countries learn as much mathematics as the best students in the United States. Data from the Second International Mathematics Study shows that the performance of the top 5 percent of U.S. students is matched by the top 50 percent of students in Japan. Our very best students—the top 1 percent—scored lowest of the top 1 percent in all participating countries. (p. 31)

These authors do not accept the point of view that we should not be too concerned with such results because educational systems differ as do the goals of education. In addition, they do not accept the reasoning that the content of a curriculum is a matter of choice, with such choices involving tradeoffs among competing goals.

When looking at math test results from their 1980 and 1987 studies, the authors concluded that Japanese children showed consistently superior performance from kindergarten through fifth grade. They further concluded that the inferiority of U.S. children compared to Japanese children obviously begins early and grows worse as pupils pass through elementary school. Chinese children, on the other hand, perform not much better than U.S. children in kindergarten, but thereafter they show rapid improvement in their scores. The authors' contention is that our culture (or at least our U.S. society) "conditions" each of us to view reality in a particular way, an echo of Nobles's definition of culture cited earlier. For example, when children in Beijing and Chicago evaluated the importance of factors such as "effort" and "ability" in terms of school achievement, the results showed some degree of similarity in the area of "ability" but a marked difference in the area of "effort," with the Chinese children giving much more importance to "effort."

It can be argued that the way people think about "effort" and "ability" affects the way they think about learning. In the Unites States, for example, students whom we label "bright" (or highly able, or gifted, or honor students) are expected to "get it," whereas we label others as "slow" (often covertly) and *do not expect them to "get it."* In this way of viewing the world, a child's motivation to try hard is linked closely with his or her assessment of whether he or she has the ability to succeed. This is in contrast to the Japanese or Chinese notion, however, where "effort" plays a much more important role. In this view, learning is perceived to be gradual and incremental, something that almost by definition must be acquired over a longer period of time. Here, no matter what one's level, there is someone at the next higher level to be challenged, and one always has a chance of winning. Students who are better challenged are motivated to higher achievement.

Achievement is gradual and, theoretically at least, available to anyone. Asians seem to disregard the limitations imposed by an "ability" model, but unfortunately many U.S. curricula seem to buy into the notion that we need to concentrate our efforts on the students who have "natural talent and ability," thereby spending less time with the slower or even the average U.S. child. Also unfortunate is the fact that high numbers of African-American and Hispanic students are placed in the latter groups.

Identifying Solutions

In summary, it can be stated that while culture does not "cause" an individual to act or react in a certain prescribed manner, it shapes and guides his or her behavior. It also serves as a measuring stick for judging the correctness or appropriateness of a given action or reaction. Knowing how to act and learning one's basic values, beliefs, and habits generally takes place in one's family and community. Learning rules and regulations generally takes place in society at large and in schools in particular.

For too many black students, school is seen as a place where they learn of how little value they are. If achievement is to be increased for many of these students, four conditions that Steele (1992) identified must be met.

- Whatever the teacher thinks is important must become important to the student. Escalante (1992), Collins (1982), Hilliard (1990), Treisman (Karelis 1993) and many others have shown that students achieve when teachers "connect" with them.

- Teacher expectations must include challenging levels of achievement, but not frustrating ones. When students are valued and challenged, they tend to succeed.

- Contact with other cultures and their ways of viewing the world has an obvious enriching value for all students and must be a part of the educational process. The dual (and sometimes triple) cultures in which African-American students must live sometimes make the challenge of straddling several cultures a major hurdle over which some students simply cannot jump, at least not without a great deal of encouragement and support.

- African-based content must become a part of the U.S. school curriculum at all levels. As Ralph Ellison has put it, the true test of democracy "is . . . the inclusion—not assimilation—of the black man" (Steele 1992: 78).

At the First National Conference on the Infusion of African and African-American Content in the School Curriculum, Nobles (1992) stated that "we can begin a process or an educational movement wherein educators can engage in a program of activity that systematically and passionately examines, develops and implements solutions to the education crisis of African-American children" (p. 22). We have a ray of hope in his work and in other work done at the Center for Applied Cultural Studies and Educational Achievement, a university-based educational research, development, and training center devoted to the identification, explication, and application of culturally consistent educational pedagogy relative to African-American educational excellence. Let us in foreign languages not remain oblivious to what other professionals are beginning to take for granted. We need to begin where we are in the matter of cultural roots and academic achievement, but not stay there, as the African proverb suggests.

Notes

1. U.S. society has changed its position on identifying students' ethnic or cultural background at various periods in our history. The current popular stance is to refrain from highlighting a student's cultural or ethnic background. One problem with this position from the perspective of some groups is that it ignores the essence of an individual's identity. So, while many teachers with good intentions may say, for example, "I do not look at my students in that way" (namely as being African-American, Hispanic, Asian, etc.), the rest of society does, in fact, pay attention to these categories. This is an area that the foreign language profession has, by and large, not addressed in a direct manner, although there are some current efforts to deal with questions relating to ethnicity and foreign language study. These have included the AATG committee on minorities in German studies, the many Spanish for Native Speakers initiatives and publications, and the ACTFL Special Interest Group (SIG) on Foreign Language Study and the African-American Student.
2. ACTFL has had a special interest group, Foreign Language Study and the African-American Student, since 1990. The group meets at the ACTFL annual meeting, has a newsletter, and regularly sponsors sessions at the annual meeting on topics of interest to its members. Any ACTFL member can become a member of the SIG by writing to Dr. Charles R. Hancock, Foreign Language Education Program, The Ohio State University, Room 249 Arps Hall, 1945 High Street, Columbus, Ohio 43210.
3. Uri Treisman's work with minority students in math and sciences has tremendous potential for other disciplines, including foreign languages. A FIPSE-sponsored lecture that describes the project, *Academic Perestroika: Teaching, Learning and the Faculty's Role in Turbulent Times,* is available upon request from Dr. Uri Treisman, Dana Center for Mathematics Education, National Sciences Annex 1202, Austin, TX 78712.

References

Akbar, Na'im. 1985. *From Miseducation to Education.* Jersey City, NJ: New Mind.

Brice-Heath, Shirley. 1989. *Ways with Words: Language, Life, and Work in Communities and Classrooms.* Cambridge, Eng.: Cambridge Univ. Press.

Clark, Richard. 1983. *Family Life and School Achievement: Why Poor Black Children Succeed or Fail.* Chicago: Univ. of Chicago Press.

Collins, Marva, and C. Tamarkin. 1982. *Marva Collins' Way.* Los Angeles, CA; Jeremy P. Tarcher. [ERIC 328 629]

Collison, Michele N.-K. 1987. "More Black Men Choosing Not to Go to College." *The Chronicle of Higher Education,* Dec. 9.

Escalante, Jaime. 1992. "El más famoso profesor de matemáticas de la nación nos pone al día," in *El Tiempo Latino,* Spring: 23.

Hale-Benson, Janice. 1988. *Black Children: Their Roots, Culture, and Learning Styles.* rev. ed. Baltimore: Johns Hopkins Univ. Press.

Haskins, James. 1992. *One More River to Cross: The Stories of Twelve Black Americans.* New York: Scholastic.

Hillard, Asa G. 1989. "Teachers and Cultural Styles in a Pluralistic Society." *NEA Today* 7,6: 65–69.

———. 1990. "Teacher Education and the African-American Student," pp. 7–24 in Charles Hancock, ed., *Needed Research in Educating African-Americans.* Columbus: Ohio State Univ.

Karelis, Charles H. 1993. *Lessons Learned from FIPSE Projects II.* Washington, DC: U.S. Department of Education.

National Research Council. 1989. *Everybody Counts: A Report to the Nation on the Future of Mathematics Education.* Washington, DC: National Academy Press.

Nobles, Wade W. 1987. *African-American Families: Issues, Insights and Directions.* Oakland, CA: Black Family Instructional Publications.

———. 1990. "The Infusion of African and African American Content: A Question of Content and Intent," pp. 22–33 in Asa G. Hilliard *et al.,* eds., *Infusion of African American Content in the School Curriculum.* Detroit: Aaron Press.

Stevenson, Harold W., and James W. Stigler. 1992. *The Learning Gap: Why Schools Are Failing and What We Can Learn from Japanese and Chinese Education.* New York: Summit Books.

Steele, Claude M. 1992. "Race and the Schooling of Black Americans." *The Atlantic Monthly,* April, pp. 68–78.

Villegas, Ana Maria. 1991. "Culturally Responsive Pedagogy for the 1990s and Beyond." Trends and Issues paper No. 6. Washington, DC: ERIC Clearinghouse on Teacher Education. [ED 339 698]

3
The At-Risk Student in the Foreign Language Classroom

Audrey Heining-Boynton
The University of North Carolina at Chapel Hill

Although the economic theme song for education these days could be "Plenty o' Nothin'," we do have an abundance of educational initiatives. "Multicultural education," "outcomes-based education," and "teaching across the curriculum" are but a few of the buzz words that are causing some educators' heads to spin. Some wish they could return to the days when teachers entered a room and delivered instruction on their subject area, period. Now, along with presenting a lesson on the *pretérito* versus the *imperfecto,* foreign language educators must consider, among other issues, the restructuring of their schools, alternate means of student assessment, and site-based management. Still another educational issue to be considered is the at-risk student.

What does it mean when a school determines a student to be "at risk?" How prevalent are at-risk students? What is the responsibility of foreign language educators with the at-risk student? This article will begin with a definition of *at risk* and follow with an in-depth exploration of the characteristics of at-risk students and the indicators that can help teachers identify at-risk students. Next, the article will explore the involvement of foreign language educators with at-risk students. Finally, there will be suggestions on how to accommodate and teach the at-risk student most effectively.

Defining and Identifying the At-Risk Student

The definition of *at-risk student* given by most educators and authors is "the student who is at risk of failing."[1] Others will include the qualifier, "and who is in danger of dropping out of school." The state of North Carolina defines *at risk* as "youth who are at risk of emerging from school unprepared for further education or the kind of work there is to do" (Legislative Research Commission 1993: 4). In the past we labeled these students "educationally disadvantaged" or "educationally deprived." Professionals coined the term *at risk* in 1983 (Crosby 1993: 599).

Many researchers maintain that at-risk children are created by society. A changing economy and the shifting racial and ethnic landscape are two elements that work to put students at risk. For example, economic shortcomings have caused racial and ethnic groups to compete for fewer resources than were available in the past. Also, as Eitzen (1992: 588) points out, the changing structure of the family has affected the future of the at-risk student. In addition, changing government policies have affected them. During the Reagan years alone, government programs for the economically disadvantaged shrank by $51 billion. According to Wehlage and Rutter (1986), the most important indicator of at-risk students is low socioeconomic class. Other demographic factors that are strong predictors of dropping out of school are a single-parent family, a large family, living in a city, and living in the urban or rural South. Low expectations for good grades or success on the part of the students also lead to dropping out.

Many children are born with conditions that put them at risk. For example, a modest estimate of children exposed to illicit drugs at birth is 11 percent of live births. Consequent medical complications in these children can result in deformation of major organs. There also is a high probability that the infant will be premature and become at risk for auditory and visual problems and ongoing medical problems such as frequent colds, recurrent ear infections, and stuffy noses. Such developmental problems translate into self-regulation problems. Children with these symptoms demonstrate difficulty adjusting to transitions during the day. They experience motor difficulty that can affect their writing or speaking and frustration that can cause the student to "act out" or misbehave.

Additional environmental influences such as the parents' continued drug use may create a home setting that is not caring or nurturing (Tyler 1992). Children themselves may be drug-damaged. Teachers must be aware of symptoms of drug-damaged children: attention deficit disorder (the child has difficulty concentrating and is easily distracted); hyperactivity (the child is unable to sit still, to be quiet, or to control movements); poor coordination (the child is clumsy and unable to control crayons, scissors, or other instruments that require some level of manual dexterity); low tolerance level (the child is easily frustrated by tasks and gives up quickly); unpredictability (the child has mood swings and temper tantrums); and poor memory (the child has trouble following three-step directions).[2] These students require structure in their learning environment (Gregorchik 1992).

Researchers have determined that it takes more than a single factor to place a child at risk; the factors must be multiple and interacting (Schorr and Schorr 1988). Some factors that commonly appear simultaneously in at-risk students are low birth weight, vision defects, and living in a single-parent environment. What is of greatest concern to educators is that at-risk children come to school ill-prepared and unable to master fundamental academic skills (Schorr and Schorr 1988: 29).

Some startling figures indicate the degree to which students are at risk. O'Neil (1991) reports that 20 percent of all children in the United States live below the poverty line. Forty-four percent of black children live in poverty, and 87 percent of black children under the age of three in families headed by never-married women live below the poverty line. Nearly one in five children between the ages eight and seventeen (i.e., 10.2 million) experiences one or more developmental, learning, or emotional disorders. Prenatal drugs, divorce among their parents, and low birth weight are among the factors linked to these figures. Six percent of thirteen- to nineteen-year-olds report having attempted suicide, and another 15 percent said they have "come very close to trying." The suicide rate among youth has tripled in the last thirty years, a distressing sign of hopelessness among our youth.

Other disturbing figures abound. For example, on any given day in some city high schools, four out of ten students are absent. The dropout rate in Philadelphia is 38 percent, 43 percent in Boston. Nearly half of all Mexican-American and Puerto Rican students drop out. In 1984, over 50 percent of Chicago students failed to graduate, and only one-third of those who did were reading at the twelfth-grade level (Boyer 1987). O'Neil (1991) quotes statistics from the National Center for Health Statistics showing that every day in the United States, 1,849 children are abused, 1,375 teenagers drop out of school, 2,407 children are born out of wedlock, 6 teenagers commit suicide, 9 children die from gunshot wounds, and 107 babies die before their first birthday. Boyer (1987: 2) concludes that "the breakup of the home, communities wrenched by crime, poverty, and the loss of good teachers threaten to overwhelm our most troubled schools." We should be concerned for our economy and our national security. These children, upon becoming adults, drain our economy in welfare and social service costs because of their inability to maintain the traditional family unit. For example, in 1973, 60 percent of young men could support a family of three and keep them out of poverty; in 1984, that figure dropped to 42 percent (Schorr and Schorr 1988: 8).

The worst-case scenario for at-risk students is that they lose hope and drop out of school. What are the danger signs that identify students who are greatly at risk of failing and dropping out? One is that these students lag behind in grade level and are older than their classmates. Students who have failed one grade are 50 percent more likely to drop out of school; those who have failed more than once are 80–85 percent more likely to drop out (Legislative Research Commission 1993).

Another warning sign is that their academic performance is low. For example, the National Longitudinal Survey reported that a majority of all dropouts (50.3 percent) scored in the bottom 20 percent on tests of basic skills. At-risk students dislike school and spend a disproportionate amount of time in detention and suspension. Although minorities represent 25 percent of the school population, they constitute about 40 percent of all suspended and expelled students. Hahn and Danzberger (1987: 19) report that the most common reason for girls of any race to drop out is pregnancy, which accounts for four out of five girls who leave school.

Another societal cancer affecting a child's academic future is physical and sexual abuse. Children of violence have unrealistic expectations and physical restrictions placed on them by their parents, expectations and restrictions that prohibit them from exploring the world and acquiring an emergent sense of competence. These children perceive that they have a low impact on the world and their surroundings, and they do not have the opportunity to practice goal setting. They also have difficulties with delayed gratification. As Craig (1992: 70) indicates,

> Living with violence inhibits the cognitive processes by which a child develops an awareness of self. They learn not to express their preference and make choices until they discover the mood of the offending parent. The price they pay is an absence of feeling and a sense of incompetence that stem from an inability to define the boundaries of self and thereby to experience self-control.

Abused children often are timid, fear strange places, and are afraid to take risks. These children often have difficulty focusing on the content of language, since the nonverbal language of the home is what they have learned to attend to the most. Craig continues, "Before they can be expected to function in an educational environment that assumes individual responsibility for learning, they must be taught that what they do actually affects what happens to them" (p. 70).

Another group of students with a high risk for dropping out are disadvantaged minorities who are having a difficult time coping with family problems. They are often incorrectly placed in classes for the learning disabled. Those who are misdiagnosed accept that they have a learning disability when, in reality, they do not. Language difficulties may add to the minority student's problems. For example, school districts may place limited-English-proficient students in remedial classes across all content areas. In fact, what these students need are intensive lessons in English (Hahn and Danzberger 1987).

Still another group at risk is the large number of children from privileged families who suffer from boredom, low self-esteem, and a lack of motivation. Wealth insulates these individuals from challenge, risk, and consequences for their actions. Friedman (1986) points out that these children, as do the children from poor- to moderate-income families, have access to drugs, alcohol, and sex.

Up to this point, this discussion has explored the characteristics and causes of the at-risk population, with the reality being that a number of these students drop out of school. The majority of students who lose hope in our educational system leave school between the ages of seventeen and eighteen. By the time they reach adolescence, these children bear a history of uncertainty about their future. Prevention programs that start in the junior and senior years of high school are probably too late.

At-Risk Students in the Foreign Language Classroom

This paper is based on two premises:

1. Foreign languages are (should be) an integral part of the K–12 core curriculum.
2. Foreign language study is (should be) for all students.[3]

Not all foreign language educators hold these beliefs, however. Many foreign language teachers, as well as administrators and teachers from other content areas, do not view foreign languages as a part of the core or "regular" curriculum. The perception is that foreign languages are a frill or that they are a skill area that only a few can master and should pursue. Our discipline is viewed as belonging to another stratosphere that has little relevance to the basics and the here and now. We are sometimes guilty of fueling this notion ourselves by not insisting on taking leadership roles in curriculum development, school government, and school policy decisions. We have allowed other content areas to dictate our role as a secondary one in the schools.

Not all K–12 foreign language teachers, especially at the high school level, believe that foreign languages are for all students. There is a contingent of foreign language educators who are elitist in their approach. "Give me your best and brightest," is their motto. They proclaim these feelings for a variety of reasons. Some just simply believe that foreign languages should be reserved for the intelligentsia of our society. Others have been unsuccessful in motivating or understanding average or below-average students, who have caused them additional work in the form of continuous discipline and the need to grade what the teacher sees as consistently unacceptable quality on assignments or tests. Many teachers complain about low enrollments; in effect, the message they send, consciously or unconsciously, offers an invitation only to students with grade averages of A or B.

Whatever the reasons, our profession cannot afford to continue with an elitist attitude. In essence, we are excluding from 25 percent to over 80 percent of an audience who can benefit in a variety of ways from a foreign language learning experience. Whether its purpose is to build foreign language skills to be used in the job world, to increase their knowledge and understanding of other people and cultures, or to reinforce previously presented information in the target languages, foreign language study is indeed for all students of all ages.

Ways of assisting the at-risk student to have a successful educational experience must be considered. A number of the suggestions involve the entire school in the solution. This points out the need for the foreign language teacher to play a proactive role in the life and well-being of the school itself. When particular teaching strategies are discussed, foreign language teachers will discover that all the techniques we consider "just plain ol' good teaching" are the very ones that work best for the at-risk student.

Assisting, Supporting, and Accommodating the At-Risk Student

It is obvious that the at-risk situation is a critical and pervasive one that has permeated our society. Equally obvious is the fact that our schools are not to blame for the economic and familial woes of society. Nevertheless, our schools must play a vital role in achieving a solution. One problem has been, though, that the curricula of our schools have not met the needs of at-risk students. Schools have overemphasized "the basics" and encouraged the teaching of discrete skills presented in a linear sequence. Students rarely practice application, analysis, synthesis, or evaluation of facts. In the past, teachers of at-risk students have divided each task into smaller pieces with little integration of the whole range of skills. Students may not see the whole for the parts. One example of this would be drilling the multiplication tables without putting them into practice. Another is conjugating verbs in the foreign language class outside any meaningful context (Means and Knapp 1991: 283). As educators we have tended to ignore the teachings of the philosopher John Dewey, who instructed us that all students come to educational experiences with prior knowledge. It is our duty as educators, therefore, to access that prior knowledge and begin instruction where the students are, not where we think they are or wish they were.

What can schools and, in particular, foreign language teachers do to reverse the downward spiral of the at-risk student? Ineffective schools that are not meeting the needs of their at-risk students send out young people who are ill-equipped to cope and compete in a technologically demanding society. They are untrained and marginally literate (Leake and Leake 1992). The myth is that these are exclusively problems of the inner city or of minorities. The truth is that all schools have students who are at risk of not succeeding for a variety of reasons.

What should a school system do? What part can the foreign language teacher play? The solutions involve

1. Administration and organization
2. Teacher attitude
3. Student attitude
4. Curriculum (Wehlage et al. 1987: 71–73)

Effective remediation of at-risk students demands strong and effective school administrators. There is a positive correlation between strong leadership on the part of the principal and success of at-risk students (Brandt 1987). Effective principals are able to develop and implement successful programs for at-risk students, whereas weak administrators may only talk about what needs to be done. Also, teachers' perceptions of their work environment significantly affect the effectiveness of the teacher and student learning (Brandt 1987). When teachers are positive about their jobs and their school settings, they are more successful as teachers in providing positive learning experiences for their students.

Firestone (1989) discusses the close tie between the attitudes of teachers and students. When the bond turns sour, the "alienation cycle" occurs. He describes this phenomenon as occurring when students and teachers "turn each other off," irritating and alienating one other. One group angers the other, and the other tends to retaliate, angering the first group. It is a vicious circle. It takes a strong principal to keep teachers from burning out, and student discontent must be addressed simultaneously.

In addition to strong administrators and positive attitudes among teachers and students, administrators and teachers must devise a curriculum that is meaningful and success-oriented. Effective curricula for at-risk students are comprehensive, preventive, and remedial. They also are intensive, and they assess student progress and adapt instruction to individual needs (Slavin and Madden 1989). Therefore, administrators, teachers, students, and the curriculum all play a vital role when dealing with at-risk students. Beyond discipline and order, respect must exist. Beyond high expectations, relevance must exist (Firestone 1989).

Finding Solutions

The first step in a schoolwide effort to solve the at-risk problem is for an administrator to provide inservice on the degree of the problem and to suggest solutions. Principals must deal with a tendency among teachers to rationalize and generalize about why they either are not dealing with or have been ineffective with at-risk students. Many teachers say "I gave it my best shot." They are uninterested in either consulting with experts or hearing suggestions on how to improve. Another typical comment is "Who couldn't be successful with a handful of students?" The reference is to special-education teachers who have the at-risk students with more severe problems. Some teachers actually resent the small class size of special-education teachers, which demonstrates a true lack of comprehension of the kinds of students assigned to special education.

Teachers also pose legitimate questions to their administrators such as "Where's the follow-through?" Many administrators acknowledge there is an at-risk problem in their school and may even attempt to devise solutions. Yet either they do not put these remedial programs into practice or they leave out important aspects, such as evaluation. Another valid question asked by teachers is "Training is important, but when?" Many principals want their teachers to improve or modify instruction, yet they do not provide the money or release time to accomplish this.

Administrators' goals of inservice are (1) to increase the willingness and capability of classroom teachers to address the instructional needs of individual at-risk students, (2) to utilize the expertise available within the school district and community, and (3) to reduce the number of students who are placed in pullout programs, receive low grades, or drop out of school. Duke (1992) points out that early identification of students is essential. Customized training within individual classrooms is critical.

Teachers who modify their instruction bring about the most success in the at-risk student. Conventional teaching is less effective for this group. Furthermore, students' homes and communities often are not conducive to or supportive of school learning (Brandt 1990). This is important for foreign language teachers to take into account, since those who do not support school learning often are not in favor of anything that is viewed as un-American (like foreign languages).

Some educators say at-risk students require more explicit instruction than middle-class students, but others warn against homogeneous grouping or what is commonly known as tracking (Scherer 1992). With tracking, which was taboo in our educational past, we deny students from all socioeconomic and academic-ability backgrounds the opportunity to experience and learn about decency and unselfishness. Once tracking occurs, the at-risk students are likely to be placed in vocational education, if they do not drop out before. Jonathan Kozol has shown that African-Americans are three times as likely to be tracked as white students (Scherer 1992). Our schools may simply be counseling students out of foreign languages if they are perceived not to be college-bound. We must inform those school officials who are responsible for placing students in courses that we are able to provide successful, meaningful experiences for all students.

Another term synonymous with tracking is *ability grouping*. As Peterson (1989) points out, ability grouping is actually harmful to remedial students. They perceive themselves as failures, since they are always paired with the "dumb" or "slow" students, and they do not have peer models to demonstrate that what the teacher is requiring is attainable. Too often, teachers, including those in foreign languages, provide opportunities for pair work or cooperative learning in their classes but pair students of similar abilities. This means that slow students repeatedly work with other slow students and do not have the benefit of learning from their more successful peers. As in all situations in life, if we are not challenged, we do not grow.

Designing Instructional Strategies

It has been shown that effective instructional strategies for at-risk students are cooperative learning, one-on-one tutoring, and individually adapted computer-assisted instruction. Cooperative learning is successful because students are able to learn from their peers, a technique we know to be extremely effective for all learners. One-on-one tutoring affords the at-risk student the individual attention required. Computer-assisted instruction is effective because it allows at-risk students to work at their own pace, in a nonthreatening atmosphere. Teachers who are most effective with at-risk students assess frequently and modify instruction based on the progress of the students (Slavin and Madden 1989).

These three successful strategies are not new to foreign language teachers. For example, cooperative learning has been a popular topic at foreign language conferences for several years. It is easy to employ in the second-language classroom and, as the research has indicated, reaps rewards not only for the at-risk students but for all students. One-on-one tutoring is also a familiar friend to foreign language educators. Most foreign language teachers meet students who need additional help before, during, and after school. Our profession needs to explore more ways to afford individual assistance to our foreign language students via student tutors, native speaker aides, and other foreign language volunteers from the community. Finally, computer-assisted instruction in foreign languages is becoming more accessible and user-friendly. Technology will play an increasingly important role in our field and will provide additional assistance for the at-risk students.

Other successful instructional strategies for reaching at-risk students include teachers working with a group of students for several years, or the same teacher delivering instruction in several subject areas (Cuban 1989). In foreign language terms, this means assigning students to the same teacher for levels one, two, and beyond. Teachers who are successful with at-risk students reshape the curriculum by (1) focusing on complex, meaningful problems, (2) embedding basic skills instruction in the context of more global tasks, and (3) making connections with students' out-of-school experiences and cultures (Means and Knapp 1991).

A false instructional assumption that has persisted too long is that learning certain skills must take place before learning others. For example, Means and Knapp (1991) cite Palinscar and Brown, who believe that learning to decode must be accomplished before one is able to employ higher-order thinking skills. A group of reading, writing, and math experts maintain that approaches that do not include higher-order thinking skills have three major weaknesses: (1) they underestimate what students are capable of doing; (2) they postpone more challenging and interesting work for too long, and in some cases, forever; and (3) they do not motivate or provide a meaningful context for learning or for employing the skills that are taught (Knapp and Shields 1990). Active learning that emphasizes higher-order thinking skills and cooperative learning, as well as mixed-ability and multiage grouping within and across classrooms, has positive effects on student motivation and learning (Cuban 1989). If foreign language educators do not employ these techniques, not only will the at-risk students suffer, but so will the "traditional constituency" of foreign languages. All students need to be able to experience the purpose of foreign language learning, i.e., the ability to communicate in meaningful contexts. Learning strategies such as higher-order thinking skills and cooperative learning provide students with opportunities to do more than name and identify objects.

Means and Knapp (1991) describe another model for what they call "new instructional strategies." They suggest development of powerful *thinking strategies,* thinking aloud while reading a text, for example, or asking oneself questions concerning how things fit with what one already knows. Encouraging *multiple approaches* to academic tasks affords several ways the at-risk student can approach an assignment. Providing *scaffolding,* i.e., breaking a complex task into parts, enables students to accomplish complex tasks by completing individual components sequentially before putting them together to form a whole. Besides thinking skills, multiple approaches, and scaffolding, *dialogue* can provide a student-centered rather than a teacher-centered learning experience. This environment affords at-risk students an opportunity to practice and rehearse what they are learning (Means and Knapp 1991). All these suggestions can be (and have been) implemented by foreign language teachers in their classroom instruction.

What Constitutes Good Teaching?

Clearly, an at-risk student requires specialized instruction. Haberman (1991) contrasts two types of teaching, the pedagogy of poverty versus good teaching. A series of teaching acts makes up the pedagogy of poverty, he believes. Teaching acts include giving information, asking questions, giving directions, making assignments, monitoring seat work, reviewing assignments, giving tests, reviewing tests, assigning homework, reviewing homework, settling disputes, punishing noncompliance, marking papers, and giving grades. Additional activities that are not teaching but are a part of the pedagogy of poverty include record-keeping, parent conferences, staff meetings, and assorted school duties such as hall monitoring, bus duty, study hall.

On the other hand, good teaching occurs whenever students are involved with issues they regard as vital concerns. Whenever students are involved with explanations of human differences, good teaching occurs. Whenever students are being helped to see major concepts, big ideas, and general principles and are not merely engaged in the pursuit of isolated facts, good teaching results. Whenever students are involved in planning what they will be doing, it is likely that good teaching is happening. Whenever students are involved with applying ideals such as fairness, equity, or justice to their world, it is likely that good teaching is occurring. Whenever students are actively involved in heterogeneous groups, it is likely that good teaching is the result. Whenever students are asked to think about an idea in a way that questions common sense or a widely accepted assumption, that relates new ideas to ones learned previously, or that applies an idea to the problems of living, then there is a chance that good teaching is going on. Whenever students are involved in redoing, polishing, or perfecting their work, or whenever teachers involve students with the technology of information access, good teaching ensues. Whenever students are involved in reflecting on their own lives and how they have come to believe and feel as they do, good teaching results (Haberman 1991).

Foreign language educators can learn much from Abdulalim Shabazz and Jaime Escalante, two famous math teachers who demonstrate year after year that at-risk students are capable of learning. Hilliard (1991) reports Shabazz's belief that it is a matter of the teacher "releasing the genius in children." He further cites Shabazz's educational goals (p. 32):

1. To teach understanding rather than merely to teach mathematical operations
2. To teach mathematical language for the purpose of communicating in mathematics and not merely as a way to solve textbook problems
3. To teach students that math is not at all a fixed body of knowledge but rather an experimental enterprise in which students attempt a variety of strategies
4. To have students believe mathematics "is nothing more than a reflection of life, and that life itself is mathematical" (Symbols used in mathematics approximate the reality of human experience and cosmic operations.)
5. To give students a sense of hope that they can become superior performers

Replacing here the word *mathematics* with *foreign languages* brings home yet again the notion that foreign language programs set the same goals and aspirations for students as do the content areas that belong to the so-called "regular curriculum."

Besides their many other roles, teachers (including foreign language teachers) must become cheerleaders and spirit boosters. Unfortunately, educators' faith in students is sometimes so low that teachers' approaches often lack vitality and do nothing to stimulate an already disheartened audience. As Hilliard (1991: 33) states, "Teachers are the mediators who provide or fail to provide the essential experiences permitting students to release their potential. The primary roles of teachers ought to be: (1) the teacher as a member of an intellectual learning community, both general and specialized; (2) the teacher as stakeholder in the community that he or she serves; (3) the teacher as community advocate and not merely as student advocate; (4) the teacher as participant in goal setting for children and their communities."

The Role of the School

Successful intervention requires early identification of at-risk children by counselors and other school officials. Counselors play an important role, since preventing dropping out of high school cannot be based solely on academic remediation. At-risk students need mentoring and counseling, social services, and remedial instruction. Hahn and Danzberger (1987) suggest that year-round schools offer a solution to fulfilling these needs, with parental involvement and school-business collaboration also playing an important role. When parents demonstrate they are interested in school, their children see the importance of education. When businesses provide support with both human and financial resources, they send a message that they care about their community and its citizens.

Besides providing strong leadership and effective inservice activities, another duty for administrators is to review the school calendar with an eye to the students' academic needs and also the working patterns of today's parents. Our school calendar was set nearly a hundred years ago when over 90 percent of all school-age children were living on a farm with two parents. In summer, children tended the crops. Less than 3 percent of today's families are on farms. Moreover, nearly one of every five families is headed by a woman, two-thirds of whom work outside the home. Nearly 50 percent of all children now in the first grade will have lived in a one-parent home by the time they graduate from high school; many of these children come home daily to an empty house (Boyer 1987). Year-round schools are one answer to this problem.

Another approach to the at-risk problem that administrators can put into effect is to reduce school and class size (Slavin et al. 1992). Personalized instruction requires that one individual teacher be responsible for no more than fifteen to twenty students. Another way to personalize instruction is through the use of classroom aides who can offer at-risk students one-on-

one tutoring, an important component to their learning process. Schools-within-a-school is yet another educational concept that supports the at-risk learner. This concept organizes a larger school into units or teams where small groups of students take most if not all their classes together. They get to know each other well and are able to turn to each other more readily for academic and emotional support. This offers the sense of family and community that these students often lack. Cuban (1989) reports from the Carnegie Foundation for the Advancement of Teaching that still another key component to successful remediation is a staff that wants to work with at-risk students and principals who support the changes in the school climate and curriculum.

Communities as well as the schools must respond to a child's life needs and care for the nutrition and general health of the child, and this must begin well before the school years. As Boyer (1987) points out, higher IQ scores, a longer attention span, and better grades in school are the positive results for economically disadvantaged children who receive food supplements during the first year of life and whose mothers receive nutritional support during pregnancy. These programs are provided by local or state agencies that usually receive local, state, or federal funding.

Research repeatedly reports that the elementary school years are critical if we want to prevent students from dropping out. Most studies advocate intervening with these children even before they begin kindergarten. Schorr and Schorr (1988) indicate that for every dollar spent on Head Start, four to seven dollars can be saved from programs that address intervention at a later age.

What are the characteristics of an outstanding K–6 school? In an interview with Brandt (1987), Richard Andrews listed twelve factors that distinguish effective elementary schools:

1. Purposeful leadership of the staff by the principal
2. Involvement of the assistant principal
3. Involvement of teachers
4. Consistency among teachers
5. Structured classes
6. Intellectually challenging teaching
7. Work-centered environment
8. Limited focus within each class
9. Maximum communication between teachers and students
10. Record-keeping
11. Parental involvement
12. Positive climate

The Importance of Reading Skills

Of all the skills, experts (see, for example, Slavin and Madden 1989) agree that reading is the key to student success or failure. Students who have failed one or more grades and are reading below grade level are extremely unlikely to finish school. Almost all children want to learn when they enter school, but by the end of first grade many have already experienced failure. Early success does not ensure total success; but early failure does virtually guarantee failure in later schooling.

We know that it is important for reading material to have relevance to what the reader already knows so that inferences can be made and the reader can make appropriate assumptions of what is to follow. Means and Knapp (1991) quote Brown et al., who report that when teachers select materials that spark an interest in reading, a desire grows to read more. This fact has strong implications for the foreign language classroom. More students, including at-risk students, will be likely to continue studying at the upper levels of foreign language if the assignments are meaningful. Selecting foreign language readings that are interesting and age-appropriate will stimulate students to want to read more.

To summarize, at-risk students pose a complex series of challenges to today's schools that demand a multifaceted approach. Solutions include

1. Collaboration and coordination of existing human and physical resources
2. The development of local ownership and commitment through staff and parental involvement in the planning and implementation of programs for students who have been placed at risk
3. Emphasis on prevention and early intervention
4. Opportunities for nontraditional educational experiences
5. Focus on the family (Legislative Research Commission 1993: 20)

Conclusions

In 1983, *A Nation at Risk* warned us of impending doom, an Armageddon sure to destroy our schools. Our schools have a number of problems that demand our attention, but one of the most critical is that of the at-risk student. These students are often identified first by poor grades that are highly correlated with poor attendance, behavior problems, and dropping out of school. Some schools doom these children from the start by tracking them from an early age. Minorities are conspicuously missing in gifted and talented programs (Oakes 1985).

For large school districts, the worry is that these needy children will become a part of a bureaucratic nightmare because departments within school systems are poorly organized with little communication. Although communities may have local agencies that could provide services, the schools do not necessarily collaborate with them effectively.

What is called for fundamentally is an increase in students' desire to learn, a boost in students' self-esteem, and enhancement of academic performance (Cuban 1989). To accomplish this, schools and teachers need to focus on course content, standards and expectations, school calendars, the quality of teaching, leadership, and fiscal support (Crosby 1993). Many techniques—such as providing structure and supervision, having appropriate expectations, setting limits, serving as a role model, emphasizing incentives and rewards rather than punishments, recognizing achievements, creating an atmosphere in which children are allowed to participate and are expected to be responsible—are ones considered "just good teaching" (Linehan 1992: 62).

In light of the changing complexion of our society over the next decade, foreign language educators need to revisit the issue of who our audience is. We complain when government reports or state or local initiatives ignore foreign language as an essential component in all students' curricula. If we truly believe that foreign language study is an integral, core component of the K–12 curriculum and an important subject for all students, then we must become active members of our school community, and that includes working toward solutions for the at-risk problem.

Besides being a part of the larger school-community picture, foreign language teachers also must evaluate their own teaching practices. It is interesting to note that all practices successful with at-risk students stated in this paper are ones that foreign language professionals have advocated for a decade as good instructional techniques for all foreign language students.

Once dedicated to participating in the solution, foreign language teachers should use the following points to evaluate problems they observe in their own students:

1. Identify the behavioral trigger for a problem behavior and develop ways to avoid that trigger.

2. Consider the context of the problem behavior. For example, the student could be consistently tardy in the morning because the parents go to work late and the student relies on them for transportation to the school. A solution might be to try to have the school not schedule a first-period class for the student.

3. Examine the function served by the problem behavior and identify an appropriate alternative behavior. For example, if a student is misbehaving, move the child to another area of the room so as to not disturb the other students.

4. Consider how the nature of the instructional process meets the needs of these children. For example, students who have been abused need the consistency and predictability of a highly structured teaching method

that provides advance organizers, modeling, and opportunities for guided practice.

5. Determine the degree of external structure needed to reduce the likelihood of problem behaviors.

6. Provide interventions across levels (Stevens and Price 1992: 20)

The hope is that all foreign language teachers will hear the call for help and be a part of the solution. Besides accepting the notion that foreign languages are for everyone, it is also hoped that foreign language educators will teach all students as they would at-risk students, that is, in a meaningful context and a nurturing setting.

Notes

1. For those who would like several sources as an introduction to educational responses to the at-risk student, this author highly recommends O'Neil (1991) and Slavin and Madden (1989).

2. The September 1992 issue of the *Phi Delta Kappan* contains excellent articles with specific information on fetal alcohol syndrome (Burgess and Streissguth), prenatal exposure to cocaine (Griffith), childhood exposure to lead (Needleman), and children with other medical problems (Bartel and Thurman).

3. This author defines "all students" as everyone except the profoundly handicapped.

References

Bartel, Nettie R., and S. Kenneth Thurman. 1992. "Medical Treatment and Educational Problems in Children." *Phi Delta Kappan* 74,1: 57–60.

Boyer, Ernest L. 1987. "Early Schooling and the Nation's Future." *Educational Leadership* 44,6: 2–6.

Brandt, Ronald S. 1987. "On Leadership and Student Achievement: A Conversation with Richard Andrews." *Educational Leadership* 45,1: 9–16.

————, ed. 1990. *Students at Risk.* Alexandria, VA: Association for Supervision and Curriculum Development.

Burgess, Donna M., and Ann P. Streissguth. 1992. "Fetal Alcohol Syndrome and Fetal Alcohol Effects: Principles for Educators." *Phi Delta Kappan* 74,1: 24–29.

Craig, Susan E. 1992. "The Educational Needs of Children Living with Violence." *Phi Delta Kappan* 74,1: 67–71.

Crosby, Emeral A. 1993. "The 'At-Risk' Decade." *Phi Delta Kappan* 74,8: 598–604.

Cuban, Larry. 1989. "At-Risk Students: What Teachers and Principals Can Do." *Educational Leadership* 46,5: 29–32.

Duke, Daniel. 1992. "How a Staff Development Plan Can Rescue At-Risk Students." *Educational Leadership* 50,4: 28–31.

Eitzen, D. Stanley. 1992. "Problem Students: The Sociocultural Roots." *Phi Delta Kappan* 73,8: 584–90.

Firestone, William A. 1989. "Beyond Order and Expectations in High Schools Serving At-Risk Youth." *Educational Leadership* 46,5: 41–45.

Friedman, S. C. 1986. "Death in Park: Difficult Question for Parents." *New York Times,* Sept. 11.

Gregorchik, Lameece Atallah. 1992. "The Cocaine-Exposed Children Are Here." *Phi Delta Kappan* 73,9: 709–11.

Griffith, Dan R. 1992. "Prenatal Exposure to Cocaine and Other Drugs: Developmental and Educational Prognoses." *Phi Delta Kappan* 74,1: 30–34.

Haberman, Martin. 1991. "The Pedagogy of Poverty versus Good Teaching." *Phi Delta Kappan* 73,4: 290–94.

Hahn, Andrew, and Jacqueline Danzberger. 1987. *Dropouts in America. Enough Is Known for Action.* Washington, DC: Institute for Educational Leadership.

Hilliard, Asa III. 1991. "Do We Have the *Will* to Educate All Children?" *Educational Leadership* 49,1: 31–36.

Knapp, Michael S., and Patrick M. Shields. 1990. "Reconceiving Academic Instruction for the Children of Poverty." *Phi Delta Kappan* 72,10: 753–58.

Leake, Donald, and Brenda Leake. 1992. "African-American Immersion Schools in Milwaukee: A View from the Inside." *Phi Delta Kappan* 73,10: 783–85.

Legislative Research Commission. 1993. *Students at Risk? Report to the 1993 General Assembly of North Carolina.* Raleigh, NC: State of North Carolina.

Linehan, Michelle Fryt. 1992. "Children Who Are Homeless: Educational Strategies for School Personnel." *Phi Delta Kappan* 74,1: 61–66.

Means, Barbara, and Michael S. Knapp. 1991. "Cognitive Approaches to Teaching Advanced Skills to Educationally Disadvantaged Students." *Phi Delta Kappan* 73,4: 282–89.

Needleman, Herbert L. 1992. "Childhood Exposure to Lead: A Common Cause of School Failure." *Phi Delta Kappan* 74,1: 35–37.

Oakes, Jeannie. 1985. *Keeping Track: How Schools Structure Inequality.* New Haven, CT: Yale Univ. Press.

O'Neil, John. 1991. "A Generation Adrift?" *Educational Leadership* 49,1: 4–10.

Peterson, John M. 1989. "Remediation Is No Remedy." *Educational Leadership* 46,6: 24–25.

Scherer, Marge. 1992. "On Savage Inequalities: A Conversation with Jonathan Kozol." *Educational Leadership* 50,4: 4–9.

Schorr, Lisbeth B., with Daniel Schorr. 1988. *Within Our Reach. Breaking the Cycle of Disadvantage.* New York: Anchor.

Slavin, Robert, and Nancy A. Madden. 1989. "What Works for Students at Risk: A Research Synthesis." *Educational Leadership* 46,4: 4–13.

———, Nancy L. Karweit, and Barbara A. Wasik. 1992. "Preventing Early School Failure: What Works?" *Educational Leadership* 50,4: 10–18.

Stevens, Linda J., and Marianne Price. 1992. "Meeting the Challenge of Educating Children at Risk." *Phi Delta Kappan* 74,1: 18–23.

Tyler, Rachelle. 1992. "Prenatal Drug Exposure: An Overview of Associated Problems and Intervention Strategies." *Phi Delta Kappan* 73,9: 705–08.

Wehlage, Gary G., and Robert A. Rutter. 1986. "Dropping Out: How Much Do Schools Contribute to the Problem?" *Teachers College Record* 87,3: 374–92.

———, Robert A. Rutter, and Anne Turnbaugh. 1987. "A Program Model for At-Risk High School Students." *Educational Leadership* 44,5: 70–73.

4

I Can't Get Them to Talk:

Task Content and Sequencing in the Advanced Conversation Class

Robert L. Davis
H. Jay Siskin
University of Oregon

Many language teachers are delighted, even relieved, to teach an advanced conversation course,[1] viewing such a class as a lightweight teaching assignment. Instructors often assume that students at this level should be able to produce utterances in the target language; the teacher's primary challenge is that of providing the opportunity and stimulus to tap into a presumed wealth of information and opinions. In this view, teachers expect students to come to the course having "covered" all the grammar of the language in the initial two years of study and assume the major impediment to students' nativelike production is a lack of vocabulary. Moreover, teachers believe that with this putative control of more grammar points comes an increased ability in carrying out higher-level cognitive processes and in performing more complex communicative tasks.

The reality is that teachers often find conversation classes at the advanced level very frustrating. Bayoff (1986) highlights several problems found at the advanced level, including students' mixed level of linguistic proficiency and uneven motivation:

> In spite of [students'] enthusiasm and almost limitless goodwill, . . . I often find conversation courses unsatisfying to teach. It is rare to have a group of students whose knowledge is homogeneous enough so that all are able or want to participate fully in debates. Those who are the most motivated automatically dominate the conversation to the detriment of the more passive who are happy to offer an occasional "yes" or "no." (p. 675, our translation)

Kaplan and Sinclair (1984) pinpoint another problem with the oral component of upper-division classes: "In traditional courses . . . students are constantly faced with having to perform linguistic tasks that require a higher level of oral proficiency than they possess" (p. 492).

The problems alluded to above point to a lack of congruity among task goal, task components, and learners' preparation. In this article, we will address this mismatch, proposing models for task design that emphasize input, skill getting, and sequencing of activities to facilitate the development of higher-level cognitive skills and their linguistic expression. We will illustrate our discussion with classroom materials conceived within this framework.

Review of the Literature

The literature contains relatively few works that treat advanced conversation classes.[2] Among them are the idiosyncratic "I-tried-this-and-it-worked" techniques, models that are not explicitly informed by linguistic or pedagogical models. Geno (1981), for example, proposes a conversation course based on the reading of Tocqueville's *De la démocratie en Amérique*. His technique involves a two-stage progression of comprehension checks: questions of a general nature are followed by questions related to specific information in the text. Although appealing, the rationale behind the choice and formulation of his activities within any linguistic or pedagogical framework is not made explicit. Furthermore, his tasks do not provide students with the tools necessary to carry out the tasks.

Bayoff (1986), as another example, proposes development of conversation skills through a five-step process leading to the production of a play. After a historical overview of French theater, students read and edit the script and undertake a series of rehearsals, culminating in a final dress rehearsal that precedes the actual performance of the work. While this innovative idea was greeted enthusiastically by students and seemed to raise their linguistic level, Bayoff's strategy has no explicit theoretical basis; at no point does she specify any linguistic or communicative goals or provide strategies to achieve them.

Another questionable aspect of these and similar courses is that they attempt to address the problems of teaching advanced conversation by providing learners with "interesting" input. This approach assumes that supplying a stimulus will automatically result in animated conversation. As Geno (1981) observes, "From a careful reading of this chapter flows a certain number of questions that will stimulate discussion in a conversation class" (p. 663), and he reinforces his claim later in his work:

The discussions and debates that can follow all these considerations lead to passionate interest on the part of students. . . . Their thought is stimulated, and after having acquired the necessary vocabulary in the preceding discussions, they throw themselves into unbridled discussion (and debates). (p. 665, our translation)

A third assumption of the authors in this group is that a mastery of grammar and lexicon will result in a functional linguistic ability. Lutcavage (1990) clearly subscribes to this point of view in the description of his advanced language course:

A prerequisite for the advanced course was the completion of a college intermediate program or equivalent preparation. The students had, therefore, *already been exposed to an elementary grammar introduction and an intermediate review*. (p. 190, emphasis added)

Thus, Lutcavage and others make the equation that "grammar plus vocabulary equals conversation." Given the insights of the proficiency orientation, it is obvious that this equation is false; oral proficiency is developed by practicing linguistic functions and contexts that are hierarchically arranged (see Omaggio Hadley 1993, for example).

Other authors embed their discussion of advanced conversation more within a theoretical framework, specifically, the proficiency orientation. In most cases, their articles follow a similar pattern: after cataloging Advanced-level functions (such as narrating and describing), these authors propose activities that ask students to rehearse the cited functions:

"Funds for the Children's Zoo" . . . The activity focuses on persuasion as a linguistic function. Students work in pairs. The children's zoo administrator is trying to convince a representative of a charitable institution to give money for the zoo by telling him or her what the zoo needs. Student One is the zoo administrator and Student Two is the chair of the fund-granting charitable organization. Students are asked to use zoo vocabulary to persuade someone to do something (in this case to give money). (Hahn and Michaelis 1986: 76)

In this and other cases, the authors' focus is on function, with secondary (or no) attention to lexical input and knowledge of content. Put in terms of the proficiency assessment criteria (Omaggio Hadley 1993), the authors privilege linguistic *function* (e.g., persuasion) over *context* (situationally appropriate usage, knowledge of lexicon and content).

Earlier, Kaplan and Sinclair (1984) had already pointed to the importance of content and the lexicon at the Advanced and Superior levels:

Juniors and seniors, whether or not they are French majors, have read extensively in French literature, history, sociology and so on; they need much more intellectual nourishment and stimulation in a language class— be it composition or conversation, but especially the latter. At the same time, students who have taken a number of literature courses may have become quite adept at supporting opinions but have lost their control of "everyday" survival French. (p. 496)

They go on to describe an experimental upper-division conversation course:

> [A] two-part course was designed. Part A (two hours a week) provided the intellectual context, in the guise of an introduction to Quebec through a text, Marcel Rioux's *Les Québecois* (*Le Temps qui court,* 1980). Oral exposés with testing by the student *expositeur* and question-and-answer sessions on the material read each week, required the students to perform accurately the functions of narrating, describing, and explaining in the past and present (and to some extent in the future), and to communicate facts and explain points of view in detail. (p. 496)

While Kaplan addresses the issue of content, her model leaves implicit the means by which functions are to be realized linguistically. She neither articulates nor sequences the acquisition of lexical and structural items needed to support them.

Likewise, Omaggio Hadley (1993) outlines the assessment criteria for the Advanced and Superior levels, specifying the relevant functions, contexts, and content. She also provides sample activities for which she specifies the level, necessary techniques, and the linguistic functions practiced. However, her few examples focus on the techniques required to execute the culmination of a presumed series of tasks; she does not elaborate how content or context are to be acquired or fleshed out.

An Examination of Pedagogical Materials

Given the paucity of attention to advanced oral skills in the literature and the inadequacies in their treatment as cited above, we now examine activities from current textbooks to give us further insight into their pedagogy.

Example 1: A Debate Activity

- Students list vocabulary to express agreement and disagreement
- Class divides into two groups, chooses debate topics: use of drugs; illegal immigrants; foreign language study; exams and grades; role of women
- Students brainstorm a list of reasons to support a given position
- One representative of each group explains its reasons to the class

- Three members of each group have two minutes to respond to the other groups' opinions
- The rest of the class adds additional reasons for supporting or rejecting a thesis

In this example, the text supplies students with a list of functional expressions in a first step. Yet it is assumed that this preparation is sufficient for carrying out the second stage, which calls for a broad command of content and lexical resources.

Example 2: Discussion Based on Reading

In this activity, students are asked to

- Study a short vocabulary list
- Read an introduction to a Hispanic author's life and works
- Discuss prereading questions
- Read a short story
- Answer comprehension questions
- Discuss opinion/interpretation questions
- Perform a word study (differentiation of Spanish lexical items with the same English translation)
- Answer more questions based on the story using the word-study items
- Do contextualized mechanical practice of the word-study items
- Write a composition: (1) rewrite the story from the point of view of a minor character, or (2) write a personal anecdote on the same theme as the story

In contradistinction to the first example, this unit would appear to privilege lexicon to the detriment of function. It assumes that a control of vocabulary results in the ability to understand the literal sense of a reading, express and support opinion, make inferences, and write.

To summarize, these pedagogical materials reveal some of the same weaknesses cited in the literature review above. Although they may provide the stimulus for the use of the target language in the classroom, students are ill prepared linguistically (vocabulary, functional expressions, etc.) and may lack relevant background knowledge (content and cultural information). Moreover, the activities themselves are not sequenced in such a way as to facilitate the execution of the tasks.

Theoretical Models of Task Design

The exact nature of the weaknesses highlighted in the preceding section becomes explicit in the light of theoretical models of task analysis. Nunan (1989) begins by defining a task as

> a piece of classroom work which involves learners in comprehending, manipulating, producing or interacting in the target language while their attention is principally focused on meaning rather than on form. (p. 10)

Based on this definition, Nunan proposes that a communicative task should contain six components: a goal, input "text" (verbal or nonverbal), and an activity derived from the input; furthermore, the task should specify the teacher role, the student role, and the setting. As a concrete example, Nunan designs a task based on a questionnaire about sleeping habits:

goal	exchanging personal information
input	questionnaire
activity	(i) reading questionnaire, (ii) asking and answering questions about sleeping habits
teacher role	monitor and facilitator
learner role	conversational partner
setting	classroom/pair work

In addition to the analysis of individual tasks, Nunan's model stresses the importance of ordering tasks: "Activities can be graded according to the cognitive and performance demands made upon the learner" (p. 118). He proposes a sequence "requiring the learners to undertake activities which make progressively more demands upon them, moving from comprehension based activities to controlled production activities and finally ones that require the learner to engage in real communicative interaction. The successful completion of one activity becomes the prerequisite for subsequent ones" (pp. 118–19). Moreover, Nunan's sequencing refers not only to complexity as determined by input and learner and activity factors, but also to the chaining together of activities according to the logic of themes and learning pathways. He refers to this notion as "task continuity" (p. 119).

Nunan's insight into task sequencing is complemented and developed further by the discussion in Breiner-Sanders (1990); she elaborates a number of sequencing criteria that should maximize the exploitation of the "hierarchical nature of linguistic development" (p. 74):

concrete	>	abstract
personal experience	>	broad issues
presentation [i.e., first exposure]	>	critical analysis

| discrete sentence | > | connected discourse to extended discourse |
| narration, description | > | argumentation, debate, hypothesizing[3] |

Using these theoretical frameworks, we can now understand the weakness of the advanced conversation exercises presented in our review of the literature and pedagogical materials above; some of the elements of a task are present, but the goals, input, and/or activities cannot be recovered from the task specification. Concretely, in the "Funds for the Children's Zoo" activity above, for example, the last three items of Nunan's task design model (teacher role, learner role, and setting) can be inferred and executed successfully by the instructor: the teacher's role is that of moderator, the learners are conversational partners with specific identities, and the setting could be a telephone call. But the role play lacks an input component (functional, lexical, or content), and as a result, the complex of activities required to carry it out fail to meet the goal of the task. The task chain is poorly sequenced and lacks continuity.

Thus, learners often "can't talk" in the advanced conversation class because instructors or materials fail to develop a coherent task chain resulting in too heavy a communicative load that leads to performance breakdown.

Model Unit

In Appendix 4A, we will present representative samples of advanced tasks, using Nunan's and Breiner-Sanders's notions of task design and sequencing as our framework. Our purpose is to provide a model for materials designers and curriculum developers (very often the classroom teacher). These materials are currently being piloted in advanced Spanish conversation courses at the University of Oregon.[4] Each exercise in the Appendix sample is preceded by indications of the elements of task design and sequencing that apply to the exercise. A parallel English translation is provided to facilitate reading the lesson plan.

Conclusion

We have analyzed advanced-level conversation materials in terms of task design, showing that many fail to specify or develop task goals, input, and activities. Others fall short in terms of sequencing and continuity. These defects result in too heavy a communicative load, often leading to breakdown. In response to these issues, we have reproduced here a conversational unit that addresses task design and sequencing and is offered as a model for materials design and curricular development.

Notes

1. In this work the term *advanced* will be used to refer to a place in the curriculum, i.e., after the first two years of language study. We will indicate the proficiency level *Advanced* with upper case.
2. With the advent of the proficiency orientation, a number of articles have appeared in the literature that target the Novice and Intermediate levels. It is natural that such attention be paid to these levels because the majority of learners in university language programs are beginners, and there was a need for activities and techniques that implemented the principles of proficiency in classroom settings.
3. Birckbichler (1989) offers a similar and not incompatible analysis of task design. She conceptualizes task hierarchies within a bipolar model in which pedagogical tasks are analyzed into descriptive "dimensions," such as mechanical/communicative, structured/open-ended, and pedagogical/authentic. Related terms like *mechanical* and *communicative* represent opposite poles of a continuum, and a given task can be assigned a position along the continuum. Based on these characteristics, tasks can be evaluated for their usefulness in achieving the desired learning outcomes.
4. Similar tasks have been developed for French; due to limitations in space, we have not presented them here.

References

Bayoff, Marie. 1986. "La Conversation par le théâtre." *French Review* 59,5: 675–80.

Birckbichler, Diane W. 1989. "Classroom Activities: A Task-Analysis Approach," pp. 60–68 in David McAlpine, ed., *Defining the Essentials for the Foreign Language Classroom*. Report of the Central States Conference on the Teaching of Foreign Languages. Lincolnwood, IL: National Textbook.

Breiner-Sanders, Karen. 1990. "Higher-Level Language Abilities: The Skills Connection," pp. 57–88 in Sally Magnan and Heidi Byrnes, eds., *Shifting the Instructional Focus to the Learner*. Middlebury, VT: Northeast Conference on the Teaching of Foreign Languages.

Geno, Thomas. 1981. "Tocqueville: Source inépuisable pour la classe de conversation." *French Review* 54,5: 661–65.

Hahn, Sidney, and Joyce Michaelis. 1986. "Classroom Activities: Oral Proficiency in Action," pp. 68–81 in Snyder, ed., *Second-Language Acquisition: Preparing for Tomorrow*. Report of Central States Conference on the Teaching of Foreign Languages. Lincolnwood, IL: National Textbook.

Kaplan, Isabelle, and Margaret Sinclair. 1984. "Oral Proficiency Testing and the Language Curriculum: Two Experiments in Curriculum Design for Conversation Courses." *Foreign Language Annals* 17,5: 491–97.

Lutcavage, C. 1990. "The Advanced German Course: A Multidimensional Approach." *Foreign Language Annals* 23,3: 185–94.

Nunan, David. 1989. *Designing Tasks for the Communicative Classroom.* Cambridge, Eng.: Cambridge Univ. Press.

Omaggio Hadley, Alice. 1993. *Teaching Language in Context.* 2nd ed. Boston: Heinle & Heinle.

Appendix 4A:

Spanish Unit: University Studies in Spain and the United States

adapted with permission from *Tertulia: Advanced Oral Skills in Spanish*, R. Davis and M. Losada (Holt, Rinehart and Winston)

TA = Task analysis (after Nunan 1989)

goal
input

S = Sequencing (after Breiner-Sanders 1990)

concrete → abstract
personal experience → broad issues
presentation → critical analysis
discrete sentence → connected discourse to extended discourse
narration, description → argumentation, debate, hypothesizing

TA	<u>goal</u>: activation of process strategies, content and lexical knowledge
	<u>input</u>: non-scripted dialogue
S	presentation of new lexical material

La vuelta de la universidad. Ignacio, un chico español, acaba de volver de Northwestern University donde ha estado como estudiante de intercambio durante un año. Escucha la conversación entre Ignacio y su padre, y de todos los aspectos universitarios de la lista siguiente, señala con una cruz los que menciona Ignacio.

estar en el primer/ segundo/ tercer/
    cuarto/ quinto año
suspender una clase/un examen
aprobar una clase/un examen
el requisito
estudios de posgrado
la carrera
la asignatura
el examen de selectividad

Back to school. Ignacio, a Spaniard, has just returned from Northwestern University where he has been an exchange student for a year. Listen to the conversation between Ignacio and his father, and from the list of university-related expressions below, put an X by the ones that Ignacio mentions.

be a freshman/ sophomore/ junior/
    senior
fail a class/an exam
pass a class/an exam
(pre)requisite
graduate studies
program of study
academic subject
entrance exam

TA	goal: presentation of functional expressions
	input: following list of expressions
S	presentation

Para comparar. A continuación lee las siguientes expresiones e intenta averiguar las palabras en negrita.

Comparing. Read the expressions below and try to figure out from the context the meaning of the words in boldface.

• Hoy día tenemos demasiados abogados. Hay **más** estudiantes en la facultad de derecho **que** en todas las demás instituciones.
• **Además** de matemáticas y estadística, estudio otras asignaturas en el departamento de lingüística.
• Este año esa universidad ha mandado a **más de** diez estudiantes recién licenciados al extranjero.
• Para entrar en algunas universidades no importa **tanto** el tener mucho dinero **como** el conocer a alguien importante y tener enchufe.

• Nowadays we have too many lawyers. There are more students in the School of Law than in all other institutions.
• Besides math and statistics, I take classes in the linguistics department.

• This year that university has sent more than ten recent graduates to work overseas.
• To get in some universities it's not as important to have money as it is to know somebody and have connections.

S	presentation of conversation management strategy ("hedges")

Cuando no lo sabes todo. Une las expresiones del primer grupo con las del segundo que tengan un significado sinónimo.

When you don't know. Match the expressions in the first group with those in the second group that have the same meaning.

1. **Tengo entendido que** no se puede fumar en las aulas.
2. **Que yo sepa**, es un instructor duro.

3. **Según me dicen**, la matrícula es cara.
4. **De lo único que estoy seguro es de que** es difícil conseguir un puesto en esa universidad si no tienes dinero.

a. **He oído que** cuesta mucho dinero.

b. **Tengo la seguridad de que** no admiten estudiantes que necesiten ayuda financiera.

1. I hear that there is no smoking in classrooms.
2. As far as I know, he is a hard teacher.
3. From what they say, tuition in expensive.
4. The only thing I know for sure is that it is hard to get admitted to that university if you don't have money.

a. I've heard that [it] costs a lot of money.
b. I'm sure that they don't admit students who need financial aid.

c. **Creo que** está prohibido fumar en clase.

d. **Por lo que sé**, es un profesor exigente.

c. I think smoking is not allowed in class.

d. As far as I know, he is a demanding professor.

TA	goal: activate background knowledge and lexicon
	input: starting point of semantic web, e.g., "asignaturas"

[Instructor's note: elicit a list on blackboard of majors and subject areas that students already know.]

TA	TASK 1
	goal: gather information
	input: lexical items from previous brainstorming session
	TASK 2
	goal: compare information
	input: results of survey
S	concrete, personal experience delivered in discrete sentences; description and comparison

¿Cuál es tu carrera? Rápidamente haz una encuesta para saber qué carreras estudia cada uno de tus compañeros. ¿Qué carrera predomina en la clase? ¿Qué año universitario?

What is your major? Do a quick survey to find out what your classmates' majors are. What major predominates in the class? What year of study is most common?

TA	goal: gather information
	input: information from preceding activity, additional input from interviews
S	preliminary transition from personal experience to broader issues

¿Quién trabaja más? ¿Quién estudia menos? Busca a tres compañeros/as de clase que no tengan la misma especialidad que tú, o entrevista a unos amigos fuera de clase, para llenar el cuadro siguiente. (Puedes añadir tus propias preguntas.)

1. Nombre y apellidos
2. Año que estudia en la universidad
3. Carrera

Who works more? Who studies less? Find three classmates who have different majors from you, or interview three friends outside of class, to fill out the following table. (You can add your own questions to the list here.)

1. Name and surname
2. Year of study
3. Major

4. ¿Cuántos años tarda uno en licenciarse normalmente en esta especialidad?

4. How long does one normally take to graduate in this field?

5. ¿Cuánta libertad tiene en elegir las clases que le gusten?

5. How free is one to choose elective classes?

6. ¿Cuántas horas semanales dedica a los estudios?

6. How many hours does this person dedicate to study?

7. Horas de prácticas en el laboratorio

7. Hours of practice in the language lab

8. Lengua como asignatura obligatoria (sí/no)

8. Language as a required subject (yes/no)

9. Requisitos de matemáticas

9. Required math courses

10. Otras preguntas

10. Other questions

TA	goal: exploit survey
	input: survey results
S	survey answers lead to comparison and analysis, dicussion of broader issues, expressing justifications, preview upcoming presentation of theme of a later content area

Con los resultados obtenidos, intenta responder a las siguientes preguntas y prepárate para exponerlas al resto de la clase:

With your results, try to answer the following questions; be prepared to report your answers to the class.

1. ¿Cuál de los entrevistados necesita más requisitos de matemáticas? ¿De lenguas?

1. Which of the people you interviewed need more required courses in math? In languages?

2. ¿Es que el mismo título (B.A. o B.S.) requiere más o menos tiempo/ trabajo según la especialidad?

2. Is it the case that the same degree (B.A. or B.S.) requires more or less time/work depending on the major?

3. ¿Cuánta libertad tiene cada uno para elegir las clases que le gustan?

3. How much freedom is each major allowed in choosing elective classes?

4. ¿Qué título tiene mayor consideración social? ¿Cuál produce mejores resultados en el mercado de trabajo?

4. Which degree is most prestigious? Which produces the best results on the job market?

TA	goal: infer new content from authenic documents
	input: realia (American and Spanish university transcripts)
S	Further comparison and analysis; addition of new content to draw students from personal experience to broader issues

Las notas. Los dos documentos siguientes pertenecen a una universidad española y a una norteamericana. Describe las semejanzas y diferencias teniendo en cuenta las siguientes características:

Encabezamiento
Notas
Asignaturas y cursos
Organización del año escolar
Exámenes

Grades. The following documents are transcripts from Spanish and American universities. Describe the similarities and differences between them with respect to the following characteristics:

Headings
Grades
Subjects
Academic calendar
Exams

TA	goal: comparison
	input: new content from previous activities
S	transition from concrete data to abstract comparison to speculation/hypothesis

Opinión personal. ¿Cuál de los dos te parece más completo? ¿Cuáles son las ventajas de cada uno? ¿Qué tipo de estudiantes crees que produce cada sistema? ¿Por qué?

Personal opinion. Which of the two seems more complete to you? What are the advantages of each? What type of student does each system produce? Why?

TA	goal: gather information
	input: realia
S	return to lower-level concrete task to integrate new, related content area that will facilitate the role plays to come

Si no voy a la Uni... ¿Cuáles son las alternativas a una carrera universitaria en Estados Unidos? Haz una lista con dos o tres compañeros de clase. Luego, estudia los anuncios a continuación de un periódico español e indica cuáles son algunas alternativas para un estudiante de ese país.

If I don't go to college... What are the alternatives to university studies in the United States? Make a list with two or three classmates. Then, study the ads below, from a Spanish newspaper, and come up with a list of alternatives for a student in that country.

[REALIA: job ads from a Spanish newspaper]

TA	goal: integration and culmination
	input: lexicon, functions, and content of all preceding activities
S	allows for further comparison, integrating content and functions of the preceding activities; connected and extended discourse

Situaciones

Role plays

Dando consejos. Imagina que eres el jefe del centro internacional de una universidad norteamericana. Hoy hablas con un estudiante de España (tu compañero/a) que no conoce el sistema de la universidad. Está muy preocupado y te hace muchas preguntas sobre las diferencias que hay en los dos sistemas. Explícale lo que debe hacer, donde debe vivir, etc., y háblale del complicado proceso para matricularse.

Giving advice. Imagine that you are the head of the international center in an American university. Today you are talking with a Spanish student who is not very familiar with your university's way of doing things. He is very worried and asks you lots of questions about the differences between the American and Spansh systems. Explain to him where he must go, where he should live, etc., and explain the complicated registration process.

TA	goal: integration and culmination
	input: lexicon, functions, and content of all preceding activities
S	comparison, debate, hypothesis, in connected and extended discourse

Estudiar en el extranjero. Eres un estudiante brillante al que han ofrecido una beca para estudiar en España durante un año. Tu padre (tu compañero/a) está en contra del proyecto. Primero, prepara una lista de las ventajas educativas y sociales de tu plan, y tu compañero preparará los inconvenientes posibles del viaje. Tú intentas convencerle a tu padre que te permita ir, comparando un año en España con un año normal en EE.UU.

Study abroad. You are a brilliant student who has been offered a scholarship to study in Spain for one year. Your father (your classmate in this role play) is against the idea. First, prepare a list of the educational and social advantages of your plan, and your partner will prepare the disadvantages of the trip. You try to convince your parent that they should allow you to go by comparing a year in Spain to a normal school year in the US.

5
Preparing Foreign Language Teachers for a Multicultural and Multilingual Society

Flore Zéphir
University of Missouri–Columbia

Teacher education constitutes an item of utmost importance on the agenda of the education community and has received a great deal of attention in recent years. The changing character of U.S. society has forced leaders in the field of education to re-evaluate the teacher-education curriculum that has so long been in place. The Holmes Group (1986) and the Carnegie Forum on Education and the Economy (1986) are perhaps the most authoritative organizations that have endeavored to underscore the weaknesses and inadequacies of traditional teacher-education models and to articulate an agenda for educational reform.[1] In their respective reports, both groups rightly assert that a competent teacher needs to master a more complex and broader body of knowledge. Hence, the crux of education reform is the redefinition of the knowledge base for teachers. The importance of teachers in society is well defined by Soltis (1987) when he writes: "No other social agent outside the family and home can claim to have a greater impact on the intentional shaping of the character and mind of the children and youth in any society than its teachers" (p. 1). Therefore, it comes as no surprise that educational leaders, organizations, and institutions are deeply committed to the task of improving the quality of this particular group of "social agents."

Response of the Foreign Language Teaching Profession

The foreign language teaching profession has responded to the national call for changes in U.S. education, and in the literature are numerous articles on the subject of foreign language teacher education (Bernhardt and Hammadou 1987; Jarvis and Taylor 1990; Knop 1991; Kramsch 1989; and Nerenz 1993, among the most recent ones). Moreover, the American Council on the Teaching of Foreign Languages (ACTFL) has very recently established a task force to develop national standards in foreign language education.[2] In 1993 it published a volume in its Foreign Language Education Series that represents "a flagship in ACTFL's teacher-education agenda" (Guntermann 1993: vii). This volume contains eight articles entirely devoted to reforms in teacher education and includes a description of provisional program guidelines for foreign language teacher education.[3] Similarly, the Northeast Conference on the Teaching of Foreign Languages has devoted several reports to the issue of foreign language education (Byrnes 1992; Jarvis 1984; Lepke 1989) and is calling, through the words of Valdés (1992: 56), for "a new language teaching profession." The American Association of Teachers of French (AATF 1989), the American Association of Teachers of Spanish and Portuguese (AATSP 1990), and the American Association of Teachers of German (AATG 1993) have developed guidelines or standards for the training of teachers in their respective languages. All these organizations recognize the need for foreign language teachers to be well prepared to meet the current demands and challenges of what Byrnes (1992: vii) calls "a multicultural world in transition."

The multicultural and multilingual nature of the world, and more specifically of the United States, is well documented (O. García 1991, 1992; Waggoner 1988). This increased recognition of the linguistic and cultural diversity of U.S. society has forced foreign language professionals to take a more progressive stance on the issue of teacher education and to re-evaluate the definition and the role of foreign language teachers. O. García (1992: 3) argues that "our task as language educators encompasses not only knowing the language and culture of the people whose language we teach, but also the language and culture of the people whom we teach." She urges teachers to become language sociologists, stating that "language educators must also be responsible for studying Sociology of Language in order to understand the position of the language they teach in the society from which it comes and to which it comes" (p. 20).

ACTFL (1993: 215) echoes a similar concern when it calls for "an awareness of the perspective of one's audiences" as an aspect of the personal development of a teacher. This perspective certainly includes the audience's own language and culture. In addition, ACTFL contends that "an essential characteristic of an effective teacher is the ability to communicate well with a wide variety of audiences." An understanding of the perspective of these audiences can certainly contribute to greater and more effective communication. Furthermore, in the area of specialist development, which includes a culture and civilization rubric, ACTFL urges foreign language education programs to provide teachers with the opportunity "to discuss, research, and reflect upon the daily patterns, societal structure, institutions, and value systems of the people who speak the language" (p. 225); and finally ACTFL stresses the importance of acquiring knowledge about the nature of language and the significance of language change and variation that occur over time, space, and social class (p. 226).

This call for cultural and sociolinguistic knowledge is also voiced by the language-specific organizations. Indeed, AATF in 1989 proposed that French language teachers achieve competency in five different areas, one of which was culture.[4] As noted by Lafayette (1993: 145), of all the foreign language professional associations, AATF is the one that offers "the most in-depth treatment of culture." This organization defines cultural competence as "a combination of three interrelated parts: the sociolinguistic ability to communicate, certain areas of knowledge, and certain informed attitudes" (AATF 1989: 14). AATG (1993: 86) recommends that teachers of German be "interculturally competent and communicate in a sociolinguistically appropriate manner." In addition, it urges German teachers to have "the knowledge, awareness, sensitivity, and ability to analyze both the home culture and the cultures of the German-speaking world." AATSP (1990: 792–93) reiterates ACTFL's (1988: 81) proposal when it asks Spanish language teachers to "explore the variability of cultural concepts within the Hispanic world (including U.S. Hispanics)." In sum, all these professional organizations strongly acknowledge the importance of sociolinguistic and cultural content in the "reformed" foreign language teacher-education curriculum.

Defining Sociolinguistic and (Multi)cultural Content

According to Wardhaugh (1992: 13), sociolinguistics can be defined as a field of inquiry that "is concerned with investigating the relationships between language and society with the goal being a better understanding of the structure of language and how languages function in communication." The importance of the functions of language has been recognized in the field of foreign language teaching, and a distinction is made between linguistic competence and communicative competence (Savignon 1983).[5] Canale and Swain (1980) identify four dimensions of communicative competence, one of which is sociolinguistic competence,[6] i.e., knowledge of the sociocultural rules of language use and the rules of discourse, as well as the knowledge of speech or dialectal variations within the target community. It is imperative for language teachers to possess a certain knowledge of the social phenomena that pertain to the language they teach. Hence, one of the responsibilities of foreign language teacher-education programs ought to be the inclusion of sociolinguistic material in the curriculum.

Seelye (1984: 26) defines culture as "a broad concept that embraces all aspects of the life of man, from folk tales to carved whales." His definition of culture includes everything people have learned to do. For R. García

(1991: 224), "culture is the complex of values, attitudes, behaviors and materials that provide humans with the sustenance for social existence." A true cultural competence, therefore, should go far beyond the narrow, traditional view of culture, which is a mere assemblage of geographical, historical, and artistic facts, to include a knowledge of the values, habits, customs, perceptions, perspectives, and world view of the speakers of the target languages.

The inseparability of language and culture has been recognized, and efforts to promote cross-cultural understanding have been strongly encouraged by scholars such as Seelye (1984), Crawford-Lange and Lange (1984), and Lafayette (1988). In the words of Galloway (1992: 97), "it is one's culture that orchestrates the range of options for the why, what, when, where, how and with whom of language in use." According to Omaggio (1986: 361), one of the reasons many teachers are afraid to teach culture is because they don't know enough about it. Another major responsibility of foreign language education programs, therefore, is to remedy this state of cultural ignorance.

Since we are preparing foreign language teachers for a multicultural and multilingual world, a broad cultural or multicultural education ought to incorporate perspectives from the various communities (including those outside the traditional, European mainstream) that speak the target languages and contribute to the richness and diversity of this world. This message is well formulated by Nerenz (1993: 160) when she writes, "Foreign language teachers must learn to design and implement curricula that are based on the acceptance and appreciation of the values and behaviors in evidence in a variety of authentic cultural contexts." This would mean, in the traditional French curriculum, for example, substantial attention to francophone communities of the United States, of Africa, and of the Caribbean. Similarly, the U.S. Hispanic, Chinese, and Japanese communities certainly deserve a place in the movement toward reforming the language curriculum. Cultural education should not be concerned solely with the study of dominant groups but should also pay attention to the subordinate groups and ethnolinguistic minorities, to reiterate García's (1992) concerns. In sum, foreign language teacher-education programs, as mandated by societal reality, should strive toward providing a multicultural education.

Multiculturalism and Sociolinguistics in the Curriculum

Multicultural and sociolinguistic materials should be included in classes taught at the undergraduate level and should not be delayed until the graduate level. Although the current tendency as articulated by the Holmes Group (1986) is to distinguish between levels of teachers (instructors, professional practitioners, and career professionals), it is strongly argued here that a minimum level of sociolinguistic and multicultural knowledge should be required of all entry-level teachers. The "syllabus of competence" developed by AATF (1989) provides insights that are useful to the discussion at hand. This group identified two levels of competence in each area: a basic level and a superior level. It is imperative to require a basic level of competence in both sociolinguistics and multiculturalism of all foreign language instructors. An intermediate level of competence could be required of the "professional teachers" (instructors who have more than an undergraduate degree and teaching experience) and a superior level of the "career professionals" (those who have completed at least a master's degree and have extensive teaching experience). Regardless of their classification, teachers should not enter the foreign language teaching profession without some understanding of the relationship between (target) language and (target) society and of the views and perspectives of the speakers of the language being taught. The realities of the present-day United States and emerging internationalism would seem to dictate such a logical course of action.

Multicultural Content

With regard to the multicultural component, several universities are now requiring a course in multiculturalism as part their general education requirements. These include Stanford, the University of Illinois, and the University of Missouri–Columbia's College of Education. All students enrolled in the teacher-education program at the University of Missouri, for example, must take three credit hours in "world/international topics and multicultural studies." Students are free to choose whatever course they want from a list that includes anything from the "History of England before the Glorious Revolution" to "Classical Mythology."

Two basic problems arise from such a "cafeteria" system of course selection. First, the flexibility in selecting "anything" from a long list of options can lead to an inappropriate choice. In other words, given the well-accepted crucial function of the teacher in multicultural U.S. society, what cultural information is most valuable to enable this teacher to serve the needs of African-Americans, Hispanics, Chinese, Japanese, and many other ethnic groups that will form the student population of the schools of the twenty-first century? The Carnegie Forum on Education and the Economy (1986: 79) states the following:

> African-Americans, Hispanics and Asians account for a rising proportion of the school population. California has now a *majority of minorities* in the first three grades of its elementary schools, 23 out the 25 largest city school systems enroll a *majority of minority students.* By around the year 2000, *one out of three Americans will be a member of a racial minority.* [emphasis added]

This description of the new U.S. context suggests that teacher-education programs should immediately eliminate the "anything goes" selection and replace it with a well-guided selection of courses dealing with perspectives on African-American, Hispanic, and Asian communities.

Second, the three-hour requirement is woefully insufficient, particularly for foreign language majors. One cannot reasonably expect prospective teachers to achieve a basic level of competence in multiculturalism after only one course. It is, therefore, recommended that the multicultural requirement be raised to at least nine hours (three courses). How can this be accomplished?

Foreign language teacher-education programs are generally arranged around three main rubrics: personal development, professional development, and specialist (or language) development (ACTFL 1993). The personal development includes a liberal arts education that generally falls under the purview of the college of arts and sciences; the professional development courses are offered through the college of education; and the specialist development is provided by the language departments. One model program could be to distribute the proposed nine multicultural hours among the three groupings. For example, a course on African-Americans, perhaps offered by the sociology department, would fall under the personal development rubric. For the Spanish major, an introductory course in Chicano literature that deals with perspectives from this Hispanic ethnic community could be included under the specialist development rubric. Finally, a course on multicultural education, offered by the department of curriculum and instruction, could strengthen the professional development component by adding a multicultural dimension.

The second model to be considered here is the "cluster model." In an attempt to provide students with general education coursework that has "coherence, breadth, and depth," several universities, including the University of Washington–Seattle, the University of Chicago, Bates College, and the University of Missouri–Columbia, are experimenting with this approach.[7] This model is designed to bring more connectedness and focus into a liberal arts education. For foreign language education majors, it is quite feasible to design specific nine-hour clusters around the theme of multiculturalism, with the participation of professors from various departments. For instance, for French education majors, one such cluster might include (1) three credits taken from a selection of appropriate courses dealing with various Francophone communities: African culture/civilization; contemporary African history; Caribbean culture/civilization; Caribbean history; Haitians in the United States; African women writers; Caribbean literature; (2) three credits taken from an appropriate selection of courses on the African-American experience: the African-American family; African-American contemporary history; African-American literature; the civil-rights movement; major African-American writers; and (3) three credits taken from an appropriate selection of courses relative to a variety of other ethnic groups: Asian regions and nations of the world; the Vietnam War; Japanese civilization; Chinese civilization; Hispanic and Asian minorities of the United States. A comparable program can be devised for German or Spanish education majors. A careful grouping of courses can ensure a basic level of multicultural competence indispensable for the schools of the next century.

It is important to note that the need for coherence and structure in the curriculum is strongly emphasized in the Holmes Group's (1986) report. The report calls for "curricular coherence" (p. 47), for "a sense of intellectual structure rather than a series of disjointed, prematurely specialized fragments" (p. 17). Furthermore, it speaks against the "sprawling and often scattered courses of study" presently offered by teacher-education programs (p. 17). The message of the Holmes Group is very clear: the current traditional curriculum needs to be better focused.

The two models proposed for multiculturalism certainly contribute to curricular focus and coherence. In the first model, the role of the academic adviser is paramount. It is incumbent upon the adviser to help students choose, from a wide range of offerings, the "best" courses for their program. In the second model, courses are already appropriately clustered, thus making the selection easier and more judicious for students.

Sociolinguistic Content

Courses in the field of sociolinguistics, when they are available, are generally offered at the graduate level. Such an arrangement prevents an undergraduate major in foreign language education from achieving the necessary, basic level of competence in this area. First, it is recommended that at least one course (three hours) dealing with the sociolinguistic aspects of the major language be added to the specialist component of foreign language education programs. A coherently designed specialty program of study for prospective language teachers should include the following components: (1) language instruction, (2) literature, (3) culture and civilization, and (4) sociolinguistics. While the first three components exist in the curriculum, the fourth is lacking. The main objective of the proposed course in French, Spanish, or German sociolinguistics is the study of the position and the functions of language in the target society or societies. In addition, an introduction to dialectal variation can be offered in this course, to conform to ACTFL guidelines (1993: 226). An in-depth study of variation phenomena could, of course, constitute the object of more advanced courses.

Second, students ought to be advised to gain general sociolinguistic information as part of their liberal arts education. For example, an existing anthropology course on language and culture or a sociology-of-language course could serve that purpose. Finally, prospective teachers should be required to take a course in English that addresses the regional and social dialects of U.S. English. It is worth noting that the cluster model proposed for multiculturalism could be applied to sociolinguistics as well. Courses that contain sociolinguistic information can be grouped together. This configuration automatically ensures for all foreign language education majors an exposure to sociolinguistic phenomena. Indeed, their basic sociolinguistic competence will entail an understanding of the functioning of language (target and native) in its social context both inside and outside the United States.

Conclusion

Novice teachers or instructors should not face tomorrow's classrooms without the ability to see reality from a variety of perspectives, those of the target as well as those of the native communities. It is important for teacher-education programs to stress the linguistic and cultural diversity of both groups. The United States of the twenty-first century requires a new breed of teachers, who, as described by Kramsch (1989: 8) are "able to conceptualize and interpret the target culture from a native and target cultural perspective, and who have a critical understanding of the particular world view espoused by natives of the target culture and of the native culture." In sum, a foreign language teacher needs to become a multicultural language teacher. In the words of Nieto (1992: 275), this process first means "becoming a multicultural person." Therefore, the purpose of a meaningful college education for the new United States ought to be students who are sensitized to varieties of ethnic and linguistic differences, who in turn can be trained to become multicultural language teachers, able to "further the democratic principles of social justice" and contribute to the shaping of a harmonious U.S. society, and ultimately of a peaceful world.[8]

Notes

1. For a more detailed discussion of various proposals on teacher-education reforms, consult Phillips (1989) and Earley (1993).
2. The ACTFL supplement to its summer 1993 newsletter describes the progress of this collaborative project with AATF, AATG, and AATSP.
3. An earlier version of these guidelines was published in 1988 in *Foreign Language Annals* 21,1: 71–82.
4. The other four areas identified by AATF are: language proficiency, literature, applied linguistics, and methodology.
5. The distinction between linguistic competence and communicative competence was made earlier by Hymes (1972).
6. The other dimensions identified by these researchers are grammatical competence, discourse competence, and strategic competence.

7. The terms *coherence, breadth,* and *depth* are cited from the University of Missouri–Columbia's general education architecture document printed on February 1, 1990.
8. These words are from Nieto's (1992: 208) definition of multicultural education.

References

American Association of Teachers of French. 1989. "The Teaching of French: A Syllabus of Competence." *AATF National Bulletin* 15, Special Issue, October.

American Association of Teachers of German. 1993. "Professional Standards for Teachers of German: Recommendations of the AATG Task Force on Professional Standards." *Die Unterrichtspraxis* 26,1: 80–96.

American Association of Teachers of Spanish and Portuguese. 1990. "AATSP Program Guidelines for the Education and Training of Teachers of Spanish and Portuguese." *Hispania* 73: 785–94.

American Council on the Teaching of Foreign Languages. 1988. "ACTFL Provisional Program Guidelines for Foreign Language Teacher Education." *Foreign Language Annals* 21,1: 71–82.

————. 1993. "ACTFL Provisional Program Guidelines for Foreign Language Teacher Education," pp. 213–27 in Gail Guntermann, ed., *Developing Language Teachers for a Changing World.* The ACTFL Foreign Language Education Series. Lincolnwood, IL: National Textbook.

Bernhardt, Elizabeth B., and Joanne Hammadou. 1987. "A Decade of Research in Foreign Language Education." *Modern Language Journal* 71: 289–98.

Byrnes, Heidi. 1992. *Languages for a Multicultural World in Transition.* Report of the Northeast Conference on the Teaching of Foreign Languages. Lincolnwood, IL: National Textbook.

Canale, Michael, and Merrill Swain. 1980. "Theoretical Bases of Communicative Approaches to Second Language Teaching and Testing." *Applied Linguistics* 1,1: 1–47.

Carnegie Forum on Education and the Economy Task Force on Teaching as a Profession. 1986. *A Nation Prepared: Teachers for the Twenty-First Century.* Hyattsville, MD: Carnegie Forum on Education and the Economy.

Crawford-Lange, Linda, and Dale Lange. 1984. "Doing the Unthinkable in the Second-Language Classroom: A Process for the Integration of Language and Culture," pp. 139–77 in Theodore V. Higgs, ed., *Teaching for Proficiency, the Organizing Principle.* The ACTFL Foreign Language Education Series, vol. 15. Lincolnwood, IL: National Textbook.

Earley, Penelope M. 1993. "The Teacher-Education Agenda: Policies, Policy Arenas, and Implications for the Profession," pp. 7–22 in Gail Guntermann, ed., *Developing Language Teachers for a Changing World.* The ACTFL Foreign Language Education Series. Lincolnwood, IL: National Textbook.

Galloway, Vicki. 1992. "Toward a Cultural Reading of Authentic Texts," pp. 87–121 in Heidi Byrnes, ed., *Languages for a Multicultural World in Transition*. Report of the Northeast Conference on the Teaching of Foreign Languages. Lincolnwood, IL: National Textbook.

García, Ofelia, ed. 1991. *Bilingual Education. Focusschrift in Honor of Joshua A. Fishman*. Amsterdam: John Benjamins.

———. 1992. "Societal Multilingualism in a Multicultural World in Transition," pp. 1–27 in Heidi Byrnes, ed., *Languages for a Multicultural World in Transition*. Report of the Northeast Conference on the Teaching of Foreign Languages. Lincolnwood, IL: National Textbook.

García, Ricardo L. 1991. *Teaching in a Pluralistic Society: Concepts, Models, Strategies*. New York: Harper Collins.

Guntermann, Gail. 1993. *Developing Language Teachers for a Changing World*. The ACTFL Foreign Language Education Series. Lincolnwood, IL: National Textbook.

Holmes Group. 1986. *Tomorrow's Teachers*. East Lansing, MI: Holmes Group.

Hymes, Dell. 1972. "On Communicative Competence," pp. 269–93 in J. B. Pride and Janet Holmes, eds., *Sociolinguistics*. Middlesex, Eng.: Penguin.

Jarvis, Gilbert A. 1984. *The Challenge for Excellence in Foreign Language Education*. Report of the Northeast Conference on the Teaching of Foreign Languages. Middlebury, VT: The Northeast Conference.

———, and Sheryl V. Taylor. 1990. "Reforming Foreign and Second Language Teacher Education," pp. 159–82 in Diane W. Birckbichler, ed., *New Perspectives and New Directions in Foreign Language Education*. The ACTFL Foreign Language Education Series, vol. 20. Lincolnwood, IL: National Textbook.

Knop, Constance K. 1991. "A Report on the ACTFL Summer Seminar: Teacher Education in the 1990s." *Foreign Language Annals* 24,6: 527–32.

Kramsch, Claire. 1989. "New Directions in the Study of Foreign Languages." *ADFL Bulletin* 21,1: 4–11.

Lafayette, Robert C. 1988. "Integrating the Teaching of Culture into the Foreign Language Classroom," pp. 47–62 in Alan J. Singerman, ed., *Toward a New Integration of Language and Culture*. Report of the Northeast Conference on the Teaching of Foreign Languages. Middlebury, VT: The Northeast Conference.

———. 1993. "Subject-Matter Content: What Every Foreign Language Teacher Needs to Know," pp. 124–58 in Gail Guntermann, ed., *Developing Language Teachers for a Changing World*. The ACTFL Foreign Language Education Series. Lincolnwood, IL: National Textbook.

Lepke, Helen S. 1989. *Shaping the Future: Challenges and Opportunities*. Report of the Northeast Conference on the Teaching of Foreign Languages. Middlebury, VT: The Northeast Conference.

Nerenz, Anne. 1993. "On Becoming a Teacher: Teacher Education for the 21st Century," pp. 159–205 in June K. Phillips, ed., *Reflecting on Proficiency from the Classroom Perspective*. Lincolnwood, IL: National Textbook.

Nieto, Sonia. 1992. *Affirming Diversity: The Sociopolitical Context of Multicultural Education*. New York: Longman.

Omaggio, Alice C. 1986. *Teaching Language in Context: Proficiency-Oriented Instruction*. Boston: Heinle and Heinle.

Phillips, June K. 1989. "Teacher Education: Target of Reform," pp. 11–40 in Helen S. Lepke, ed., *Shaping the Future: Challenges and Opportunities*. Report of the Northeast Conference on the Teaching of Foreign Languages. Middlebury, VT: The Northeast Conference.

Savignon, Sandra J. 1983. *Communicative Competence: Theory and Classroom Practice*. Reading, MA: Addison-Wesley.

Seelye, H. Ned. 1984. *Teaching Culture: Strategies for Intercultural Communication*. Lincolnwood, IL: National Textbook.

Soltis, Jonas F. 1987. *Reforming Teacher Education: The Impact of the Holmes Group*. New York: Teachers College Press.

Valdés, Guadalupe. 1992. "The Role of the Foreign Language Teaching Profession in Maintaining Non-English Languages in the United States," pp. 29–71 in Heidi Byrnes, ed., *Languages for a Multicultural World in Transition*. Report of the Northeast Conference on the Teaching of Foreign Languages. Lincolnwood, IL: National Textbook.

Waggoner, Dorothy. 1988. "Language Minorities in the United States in the 1980s: The Evidence from the 1980 Census," pp. 63–91 in Sandra L. McKay and Sau-Ling C. Wong, eds., *Language Diversity: Problem or Resource?* Rowley, MA: Newbury House.

Wardhaugh, Ronald. 1992. *An Introduction to Sociolinguistics*. Oxford, Eng.: Basil Blackwell.

6
The Semantics of Culture:
Communication and Miscommunication in the Foreign Language Classroom

Gerhard Fischer
Zentrale für das Auslandsschulwesen Bundesverwaltungsamt Köln
(Germany)

> Language does not exist apart from culture, that is,
> from the socially inherited assemblage of practices and beliefs
> that determine the texture of our lives.
>
> *(Sapir 1970: 207)*

It is well documented that the learning of foreign languages must be intertwined with the study of culture (Seelye 1991; Legutke and Thomas 1991). But even Seelye's best-selling book has had little effect on classroom instruction still operating in an educational environment that emphasizes the teaching of facts, generates lists of observable learner outcomes, and favors instructional methods that are firmly rooted in Thorndike's (1966) theory of connectionism. Recently, however, more and more conference workshops and sessions have addressed the issue of teaching culture through language. There is now recognition within the foreign language teaching community that instructional methods need to be firmly rooted in a new paradigm of teaching, marking movement toward a view of linguistic proficiency within the larger area of cultural proficiency.

Superficial translations of words and ideas from one language to another without consideration of their cultural context can often create more confusion than understanding. When language students communicate directly with their peers in the target culture, their communicative encounters must be closely monitored and directed by teachers, who create a learning environment for their students to ask relevant and revealing questions. In this context, the widely used terms *authentic communication* and *negotiation of meaning* need tighter definitions for classroom purposes.[1]

Defining the Goals

One of the declared goals in the foreign language teaching profession is to teach the proper and effective use of another language in authentic situations. Most of the time, practice toward this goal is limited to situations in the classroom. Students' linguistic survival is usually guaranteed in a learning environment that is characterized by friendly and supportive teachers as well as by other students who are all too familiar with the challenges of communicating in another language. In the classroom, both students and teachers are highly appreciative of anyone who manages to cope with the stress of finding appropriate words and stringing them together in an acceptable syntactic pattern. Many activities in foreign language instruction, however, can be no more than practice imitations of situations that resemble real-life situations in the target culture. The language teacher's hope must rest on the assumption that transfer between the "practice dialogues" and "real language use" is possible and that it will occur.

The fact remains, however, that "authentic situations" or "authentic communication" are often only extremely reduced, artificial acts of communication among nonnative speakers. They are reduced because the content level of most classroom dialogues is limited to superficial exchanges of isolated language pieces and does not reflect content that really concerns students; they are artificial because the need to communicate is usually not based on the desire to deliver a message but to "get the sentence right." The consequence is that no matter how many opportunities we give students to communicate in the classroom, we too often fail to teach them real usage of the language; we fail to teach them how to negotiate meaning and express themselves adequately.

An approach to teaching proficiency and communication that does not make a serious attempt at teaching how to negotiate meaning is still trapped in the behaviorist paradigm of structuralism. The instructor has simply moved the limits of the object of the analysis. The limit is not the sound, the morpheme, the word or the sentence any more. It is now a clearly delineated conversational or discourse paradigm. It is typically still a closed paradigm in the sense that nothing unexpected is supposed to happen and that learners and teachers will "be done" within a reasonable amount of time. Kramsch (1991: 198) points out that "textbooks now feature conversational gambits and sociolinguistic markers to be learned as items of vocabulary; authentic materials are used for behavioral training. By being taught as text, discourse has been decontextualized and is now taught according to structuralist principles of language learning."

In order to function in the linguistic and cultural environment of speakers of other languages, the second language learner must know what connotations are commonly associated with particular words, phrases, and concepts. Learners of a foreign language must attempt to reconstruct the cultural context in which a speech act occurs. Textbooks do not teach these kinds of things in any meaningful way; therefore the teacher needs to refocus on the teaching of culture to make it a functional part of the teaching of language. The most important goal in foreign language teaching is that students be able to talk to people in other cultures and understand what they are saying. True understanding, however, goes well beyond what is found in textbooks and dictionaries.

In order to prove the worth of second language learning, the teacher needs to expose students to authentic, meaningful use of the language as much and as often as possible. Since multiple trips abroad for each individual student are impossible, alternatives must be found. One of these can be a well-designed school partnership program that sees as its main goal the exchange of information in its true cultural context. Modern communication technology allows the interchange of videotapes and audiotapes as well as other, more traditional forms of cultural realia. Electronic mail (E-mail) and facsimile (fax) machines also permit students to engage in authentic and meaningful discourse. The world has indeed become smaller, and we all "meet" people in places all over the globe through reports in newspapers, on the radio, and, most forcefully, through pictures on television. If we recognize that we can now reach out to the world in ways we never could before in history, we can engage in "travel" without leaving the classroom and communicate with people everywhere.

Because cultural misperceptions and stereotypes often originate from a technical and superficial word-to-word translation, the focus on concepts and ideas can often help avoid such misperceptions. An example of an E-mail project between classrooms in the United States and Germany will illustrate how cultural "communication" can sometimes become "miscommunication."

Stereotypes and Cultural Misperceptions

When German and U.S. students participated in an E-mail communication project in early 1991, all the elements for truthful authentic discourse seemed to be in place. English students from Leer in Ostfriesland were given the opportunity to talk (i.e., send messages via computer) to peers in the state of New York within the framework of a project that was called "About

Stereotypes" (Ehrig 1991). This project demonstrates many wonderful things that can be done in the classroom. Its documentation also clearly points to some deficiencies in design and administration and shows the difficult, sometimes overwhelming task for students and teachers to "talk" to others about their cultural backgrounds. Throughout the project, students offered opinions and voiced objections to what they perceived to be misunderstandings. By the end of the project, both groups had apparently managed to reinforce preexisting stereotypes.

Most of the discussion was conducted in English. From a strictly linguistic viewpoint, the German students of English benefited more than their U.S. peers. Cultural insights were gained by both U.S. and German students, however. Classroom teachers who coordinate similar E-mail projects will arrive at a joint decision with their counterparts in the other country about which language the students will be asked to use.

The project began as a simple exchange of "information." In 1991 Frank and Joern from the German town of Leer sent an E-mail message to their U.S. "circle friends"[2] in which they listed some stereotypes they had heard from shoppers in downtown Leer. They were very careful to point out that these were not views they held personally:

> What typifies the Americans according to a poll we have taken amongst some citizens of Leer?—Here is an uncensored list of answers, Germans about Americans: Americans are thought to be nationalistic, patriotic and proud of their troops. They are quite loose, yet they vote for the Republicans. They know how to succeed, eat fast-food all the time and smoke Marlboros. One man said they were obnoxious, others said they were "cool." Americans wear funny clothes, and therefore they look like parrots. Americans love money, sports, and their flag. (Ehrig 1991, March 14)

Somehow, Frank and Joern sensed that there might be problems with this message, and they concluded by asking, "Are you annoyed by what many Germans think about you or do you like your image? Would you like to change or confirm it?"

Frank and Joern certainly did not mean to offend anyone, but they apparently assumed that in order to get an interesting discussion started, some provocation and overstatement would be an appropriate strategy. Unfortunately, the U.S. paradigm of "polite discourse" is different from the corresponding German one. In general, to be polite, praise precedes negative statements and criticism in the United States, whereas Germans tend to be more direct and to the point. German students need to be aware of this before they start communicating with students in the United States, and U.S. students need to understand German discourse patterns as well. What happened in this particular case was that some U.S. students took the "poll" very seriously. Sherri, clearly offended, replied in very blunt terms:

Just recently I read your descriptions of Americans. I realize that a stereotype is not meant to be taken personally, but the comments that were made I felt were rude. I would just like to clear it up a bit. Yes, I agree that Americans are very patriotic, we can't help it if we take pride in our soldiers and our troops that represent our country. [In] the Persian Gulf War, everybody united together. Unlike the Germans who for a time separated and were fighting each other, Americans are hard working individuals. They know what it takes to succeed. In America, there is always a way—if you want to succeed. (Ehrig 1991, April 8)

Not all responses in this project reflected such misunderstanding. Some U.S. students used the German language in their responses, (e.g., "Du hast recht mit Deiner Annahme. Amerikaner essen 'Fast Food' und sind patriotisch."), and some responded with "polls" similar to that of Frank and Joern. In general, though, the discussions ended with frustration on both sides and probably confirmed preconceived stereotypes. Joern in Leer was clearly frustrated and conceded that starting the discussion with a listing of stereotypes might not have been a good idea. He mentioned that he had been an exchange student at a U.S. high school where he did not "consider it a pleasure when [he] was walking down the hallway—and one brainless 'fellow' student came up to [him] and greeted [him] with "Heil Hitler!" (Ehrig 1991, April 19). Joern mentioned in his concluding message that he loves his U.S. family and still has some very good U.S. friends. "Nevertheless, I am critical of the States the same way I am critical of my native country. I frankly believe you should do the same thing. Perhaps one should start thinking where the prejudice comes from or if it holds any truth" (Ehrig 1991, April 19).

Joern later reiterated another stereotype, namely that U.S. high schools have low standards:

The American high schools have many advantages (for instance, they are more social, etc.) [but they] are rather low-brow and [their goal] is not the procurement of too much knowledge even if one takes more demanding classes. . . . Don't be offended, but that's my opinion, however, based on experience. It was very interesting to hear what American students think about Germany and Germans and this provided much amusement amongst most of my fellow students, even though those comments seemed much ruder than most of the comments I have sent you. However, one opinion contained some truth: Germans do not shower as much as many Americans and not all the girls shave their arm pits. All the rest was very funny but lacked truth. (Ehrig 1991, April 19)

Cultural Perceptions and Insights

What would it take to turn this exchange of cultural misperceptions into a valuable educational experience so that these students could actually learn something from one another? How can we as teachers facilitate discourse that is truly open and during which students recognize the need for the negotiation of meaning? The examples above were taken from an E-mail project for a number of reasons: They demonstrate that (1) direct communication with people all around the world is possible if we use modern technology but that (2) supervised and unsupervised direct communication via E-mail is not guaranteed to be successful.

The problem we deal with as teachers of foreign languages is the same as that faced by anyone else who teaches communication skills. In spite of a great deal of talk and exchange of information, people still do not necessarily understand one another. As long as we operate within the boundaries of one culture, which are obviously not at all identical with national boundaries, we may believe that we face the relatively simple task of passing from generation to generation the cultural knowledge necessary for felicitous discourse. Hirsch (1988) discusses cultural literacy in this way and has been successful in marketing a number of books that tell parents what their children need to know at a certain age. Shared educational and cultural experiences certainly do provide common points of reference, but there is also serious doubt whether cultural literacy can be approached only from its content. Modern societies are often multicultural, and not all members of these cultures share common views on all topics. Yet in foreign language education, we often act as if there were such a thing as a homogeneous U.S. or German or French culture. We still tend to think in the paradigm of a world order in which cultural boundaries are identical to national boundaries.

There is, however, "a German way of looking at the world" and also a "U.S. way of looking at the world." Between cultures, reference points and evaluations differ, but a similar variation of viewpoints and prejudices also exists within each of the cultures. It is simply not true that all Americans are patriotic in the way that many Germans define that word and concept. It is equally untrue that all Americans work hard and know what it takes to succeed, as stated by the U.S. student above. Labeling U.S. schools as "lowbrow," as Joern does, does not make much sense either. Many Germans would say the same thing about their own schools of today. How can we, therefore, identify the "kernel of truth" in national stereotypes? How can we determine the validity of individual views, and how can we as foreigners discern what is "meant" in real-life, authentic communication in the target culture? Joern is exactly right when he says that we should try to find out where these stereotypes actually come from.

The New Paradigm in Foreign Language Teaching: Teaching from the Bottom Up

We cannot get close to solving the problem if our teaching relies solely on a *discussion* of cultural content. As Kramsch (1991) points out, a different metaphor is needed to capture what the teaching of discourse should be. She clearly sees the need for the inclusion of viewpoints or, in the language of pragmatists, the reflections on how speakers and listeners view subject matter. This can also be referred to as the relational aspect of meaning. We need to know the whole set of connotations that speakers hold in the words they use. This is, of course, extremely difficult. We cannot approach this goal at all if we believe there is a fixed set of connotations that can be analyzed and consequently taught "from the top," i.e., lecture-style. Even asking native speakers directly about their beliefs and attitudes will not yield good results because native speakers typically are not aware of many implicit assumptions in their own culture. They are obviously the carriers of cultural connotations that are valid for a large group of people, however, and we need to be sensitive to what these connotations are.

Can the teacher approach the task of teaching culture by recognizing the diversity as well as the commonality of views and opinions within a target culture? Are there teachers who are multicultural or at least bicultural to the degree that they have adequate knowledge of all these facets? Is there a way to access the truly encyclopedic knowledge of facts, views, and beliefs in other cultures? Can culture be taught effectively and exclusively in a foreign language class when "culture" touches on so many aspects of life that are usually discussed in other subject areas of the school curriculum?

There is no simple answer to these questions, but there are areas in which foreign language education needs to shift the paradigm.

1. Students need to be taught skills of inquiry, of being able to find out what people actually "mean" when they use particular phrases or make certain statements.

2. Teachers need to recognize that their role is not merely that of a lecturer who passes on to students an easily identified body of knowledge. Teachers should be facilitators of learning.

3. There is a need to include knowledge from other disciplines when we teach culture. If culture is defined as everything that concerns people in their lives (Seelye 1991), then there are obviously concerns common to historians, biologists, and foreign language teachers.[3]

4. Communication can be successful only if both speaker and listener understand the connotations and cultural implications of language. Therefore, culture cannot be an "add-on" in the foreign language classroom but must be integrated into linguistic learning.

Negotiation of Meaning: The Student as Inquirer and Explorer

In the stereotypes with which the Leer students opened communication, Americans are nationalistic, patriotic, and proud of their troops. They eat fast food, smoke Marlboros, and wear funny clothes. The origin of some of these stereotypes is clear and can therefore be explained quickly; others are far less obvious. Marlboro commercials, for example, are still shown in many German movie theaters. If this is the only source of information that Germans have about U.S. smoking habits, then the stereotype should not be surprising. How can Germans possibly know that smoking in public places is, in general, far less accepted in the United States than in Germany?

The U.S. students in the project readily admitted that many Americans consume a great deal of fast food. However, what does this bit of information tell the Germans? Their own culture is changing quickly, and fast-food establishments are becoming increasingly popular all over Germany. In general, though, this fact is still deplored and frowned upon by many Germans as a sign of bad eating habits. An interesting project could be designed during which U.S. students are asked to find out as much as possible about German eating habits.[4] They might ask their German counterparts questions about family life and find out when family members meet and talk to one another. An analysis of answers to questions like these could put "family meals" in their cultural contexts. Many German families still look at mealtimes as a social gathering, as the time when they can talk and create an atmosphere of togetherness. One finding in such a study might be that the stereotypical U.S. fast-food eater is frowned upon, not so much because gourmets in other cultures do not consider a "Big Mac" or a "Whopper" to be food, but because they find objectionable the notion of a fast-paced life with no time for real and regular interaction at the family dining table. At the same time, it might become clear that the image of happy family life in German dining rooms is, in many cases, a culturally shared happy memory rather than a description of reality.[5] The observation that many U.S. fast-food restaurants in Germany are meeting places for teenagers will also shed some interesting light on the assumption that fast-food places are merely antisocial gathering places for the rushed and stressed masses. Playgrounds at McDonald's, for example, point to a development that responds to the needs of families with young children, both in Germany and in the United States.

Whatever conclusions and findings such a project may yield, students should develop a deeper understanding of their own and of another culture. Students themselves, however, cannot be assumed to have enough cultural insights *a priori* to be able to design such a project all by themselves. This is where teachers need to take seriously their role as facilitators of learning; they need to explain to their students the idea of implicit cultural assumptions. Rather than letting stereotypical statements go by unnoticed or unchallenged and allowing their students to accept them as valid generalizations about another culture, teachers need to ask questions that raise students' awareness. Accordingly, a project could be designed to begin with simple questions that provoke observation of facts such as

- What types of fast-food places do you have in your country, your state, your town?
- Who eats there occasionally, often, regularly?
- Which age groups go there?
- Do families go there?
- How long do customers usually stay in the restaurant?
- Do families in your community have regular meals together?

After an initial collection of observations, comparisons can be made. Results from such a survey will probably show that in both countries young people have a stronger preference for fast-food places than do older people. An interpretation of these observations, i.e., an attempt to answer "why" questions, may reveal deep insights into changes of Western industrialized societies and the interdependency of busier, more hectic lifestyles and eating habits. The project may point to ways in which lifestyles are shaped by many factors over which individual families have only limited control.

Teachers will not have answers to all the questions, nor should they be expected to. They are further advanced on the continuum of cultural learning than their students, however, and have considerable knowledge of the target culture. Their primary responsibility is to help build bridges for their students, bridges whose footings are set in both culture and language. Projects designed to facilitate learning will move both students and teachers further along the cultural learning continuum. Students from both cultures can meet on the bridge and view both the target culture and their own native culture from a different perspective. For the duration of a particular project, and perhaps much longer, students will be able to see the familiar from a distance and the new from much closer than ever before.

The examples cited from Ehrig (1991) do not document any noticeable teacher foresight and assistance. Communication between German and U.S. students took place, but there is no evidence of meaningful discourse. While students were interested in the topic to the degree that they got very upset about some things that were said, the meanings of words and cultural assumptions about some statements were apparently never negotiated or questioned. The teachers may have missed a perfect opportunity to create a great cultural learning experience. They did not see beyond the old paradigm of foreign language teaching, within which they were concerned with language *form* rather than with the *attitudes and underlying assumptions* conveyed through language. Their students seemingly showed no sophistication in examining concepts and connotations; they simply transferred words from one cultural context to another without being aware of the implications inherently necessary for the process of true understanding. The new paradigm of foreign language teaching should focus on the conveyance and exchange of thought and cultural insight *through* language rather than on the teaching of language *plus* culture. The knowledge that language and thought are interrelated (Sapir 1970) is reflected in this paradigm but can hardly be accounted for in the old behaviorist and structuralist tradition.

Other examples cited from the E-mail project could be revisited in the same way, e.g., patriotism has many expressions. "More Americans than Germans display their country's flag and say that they are proud of their country," said one student. An analysis of this observation must relate to historical events and may lead to valuable learning experiences in subject areas not connected traditionally to the curriculum of foreign language classes. Joern's observation, based on his experience as an exchange student, that U.S. schools are lowbrow, needs to be examined in the light of a comparison of the educational systems in Germany and the United States. The comparison of curricula in a German *Gymnasium* and a U.S. high school is meaningless. The student populations and the respective roles in their country's educational system are entirely different. How can students know all this? Teachers need to point to questions whose answers will lead to differentiated thinking and cultural insights.

The approach to foreign language teaching outlined above recognizes another goal, deeper insight into another culture. To obtain these insights, students need to develop a highly sophisticated use of language, one in which they can question, affirm, speculate, and, in general, understand that there is more to the meanings of words or sentences than dictionaries can give. Only if foreign language teachers facilitate truly authentic and meaningful discourse can this goal be achieved, however. The contribution of the study of foreign languages to other disciplines and to the growth of our students as responsible citizens and lifelong learners will then become more obvious.

Notes

1. The phrases *authentic discourse* and *authentic communication* are used interchangeably here to refer to the use of language to negotiate meaning across cultural boundaries. The term *negotiation of meaning* is used as "finding out about," "exploring," and "coming to informed conclusions about" the denotative and connotative meanings of words.
2. AT&T's "Learning Network" (AT&T 1991) facilitated the project in the spring of 1991. Through this network, students and teachers can join "Learning Circles" all over the world, hence the expression "circle friends."
3. Seelye says, "Culture is seen to include everything people learn to do." I believe that the concept of "culture" needs to be defined in broad terms. It cannot be restricted to observable actions.
4. For an interesting example of a project in French, see the following article in this volume by Jayne Abrate, "Authentic Communication via Minitel: Pairing French and U.S. High School Students to Study Culture."
5. An extremely interesting study by a group of German researchers, the "Tübinger Modell einer integrativen Landeskunde" [Tübingen Model of Integrated Cultural Studies] (Mog 1992), provides many insights to the teaching of German culture. One of the observations regarding eating habits and meals fits in very well with my remarks: "Die ehemals geheiligte Tradition des deutschen Mittagessens ist somit endgültig mehr Ideologie als Wirklichkeit" [What used to be the almost sacred tradition of German mealtime is thus more ideal than real].

References

AT&T Learning Network. 1991. *Connect Your Classrooms with an Exciting World of Learning.* Parsippany, NJ: AT&T.

Ehrig, Detlef, ed. 1991. "Places and Perspectives: About Stereotypes." Leer, Ger.: Ubbo-Emmius-Gymnasium. [Unpaged description of project and dated collection of E-mail correspondence.]

Hirsch, E. D., Jr. 1988. *Cultural Literacy: What Every American Needs to Know.* New York: Doubleday.

Kramsch, Claire. 1991. "The Order of Discourse in Language Teaching," pp. 191–204 in Barbara F. Freed, ed., *Foreign Language Acquisition Research and the Classroom.* Lexington, MA: D.C. Heath.

Legutke, Michael, and Howard Thomas. 1991. *Process and Experience in the Language Classroom.* New York: Longman.

Mog, Paul, ed. 1992. *Die Deutschen in Ihrer Welt. Tübinger Modell einer Integrativen Landeskunde.* Munich, Ger.: Langenscheidt.

Sapir, Edward. 1970. *Language.* London, Eng.: Rupert Hart-Davis.

Seelye, H. Ned. 1991. *Teaching Culture. Strategies for Intercultural Communication.* Lincolnwood, IL: National Textbook.

Thorndike, Edward L. 1966. *Human Learning.* Cambridge, MA: M.I.T. Press.

7
Authentic Communication via Minitel:
Pairing French and U.S. High School Students to Study Culture

Jayne Abrate
University of Missouri–Rolla

In foreign language pedagogy, trends, methodologies, strategies, and techniques, both old and new, continue to vie with one another for the teacher's time and loyalty. Terms such as new technologies, communicative activities, authentic materials, contextualized learning, cooperative learning, and proficiency fill the literature; advice and practical examples abound at professional conferences. Although innovative ideas and materials may prove stimulating at first, harried classroom teachers often have trouble sustaining their enthusiasm and implementing them over the long term. One way of successfully engaging students' interest combines a new technology (Minitel) and a communicative activity (correspondence) to produce a student survey (authentic materials) that may be used to study cultural similarities and differences (contextualized learning) and promote increased spoken interaction through small-group work in the classroom (cooperative learning) and written exchanges with the foreign students (developing proficiency). This Minitel activity provides materials for students and suggests tasks for them to perform. More significantly, it incorporates authentic communication via Minitel with an in-depth examination of culture.

Background

Greater cultural understanding constitutes an important goal of foreign language instruction, since culture provides the context that makes comprehension and communication possible. Culture can no longer be considered simply a fifth element along with reading, writing, listening, and speaking. It is essential to mastering each of the four skills. Proficiency in a language requires knowledge of the cultural and social context in which an exchange takes place. Too often cultural presentations in elementary and intermediate textbooks remain sketchy, disjointed, and superficial; moreover, relatively few students receive firsthand exposure to the culture.

Students enjoy using the language in real situations. Much classroom communication revolves around role-play and other imaginary contexts. Pen pals have long been a popular function that serves to encourage interaction with a native speaker, and teachers in most languages benefit from services that match students to foreign pen pals. Unfortunately, mail is slow, and eager correspondents frequently wait months for a reply that sometimes never arrives. Thanks to today's new technologies and electronic mail services, international communication can be nearly instantaneous. French Minitel services provide one vehicle for such contact.

Originally developed as an on-line telephone directory, Minitel has grown at a phenomenal rate since the first experimental trials in 1981. Users may now consult more than 20,000 services, including shopping, publicity and information, banking, business, databases, and electronic mail services, to name only a few. Because Minitel was designed for the general public, ease of access and reasonable cost represent important features. Among the services available is EDUTEL, offered by the French Ministry of Education. In addition to information about all aspects of the educational system (structure, programs of study, exam results), it also provides electronic mail services. Any French or North American high school can request a mailbox to correspond with other schools. A new service called FRANCEMONDE furnishes its own international electronic mail network but also allows access to EDUTEL and numerous other services at a cost of 19 cents per minute. When a U.S. class is paired with a French class, students can compose and send a message via EDUTEL or FRANCEMONDE one day and receive an answer in class the next. Direct on-line links and teleconferences offer additional possibilities for contact.[1] The rapidity with which messages can flow back and forth motivates students and provides incentive for using and perfecting language skills.

A Class Correspondence Project

Minitel's high-speed international communication can be a vehicle for culturally authentic activities and materials, thus creating a fertile ground for the introduction of a serious and more-than-anecdotal study of culture, even at elementary levels. The class correspondence project described here offers a model for integrating language practice and cultural study. Conceived within the framework of a Minitel research proposal on French cuisine,[2] the project sought to have French and U.S. high school students produce documents in their native languages that, when exchanged, could be used in the foreign language classroom as authentic cultural materials and address three main objectives: (1) to stimulate conversation and reading in the classroom; (2) to develop awareness of the other culture; and (3) to promote, when possible, written exchanges through Minitel. The results, in all respects, surpassed expectations and provided the additional benefits of making students more observant of their own culture and increasing their awareness of nutrition.

The topic chosen, a survey of the eating habits of French and U.S. high school students, suited a wide range of ages and abilities. Two U.S. high school classes studying French in rural Missouri joined with two high school classes studying English in Tours, France.[3] Identified only by age and sex, a total of 98 students (64 U.S. and 34 French) completed a simple form during the two-week period from February 15 to 28, 1993.[4] Instructions called for participants to note everything they ate or drank and the place and time of day that they ate or drank. The forms were then returned to the author for analysis and copies were distributed to the students' teachers.[5]

Results

Since this study was intended specifically as a class activity, statistical design was not strict, thus limiting the conclusions that can be drawn. For instance, the majority of French students were male (23 male, 11 female), while the Americans were primarily female (49 female, 15 male). The French group was from a large city, the Americans from a rural area. The French classes were on average two years older (17.6 years of age as opposed to 15.7 for the Americans). Many of the French students boarded at school during the week and, therefore, all ate the same meals in the school cafeteria. Because of this, the dates were chosen so that the second week of the survey coincided with the French February vacation. The Americans should have been in school both weeks, but a blizzard caused them to miss four days of school the first week. Despite these difficulties, the consistency of overall responses for each nationality proved striking, and the fascinating results confirmed numerous stereotypes about French and U.S. eating habits.

French students consumed a great variety of foods: meats (including wild boar, horsemeat, *charcuterie,* organ meats, veal, lamb, mutton, and several kinds of fish, as well as chicken, beef, and pork), many different fruits and vegetables (kiwis, plums, grapefruit, spinach, lentils, beets, and endives), significantly more servings of dairy products (especially cheese, of course, and yogurt), and few soft drinks; they rarely skipped meals or ate in restaurants and had few between-meal snacks except for an afternoon *goûter*. Several drank wine, beer, and *apéritifs*. They ate at a regular time each day, even while on vacation.

The Americans, on the other hand, ate at any time of the day or night, making it difficult to categorize items as meals or snacks. They consumed large quantities of junk food (chips, cookies, crackers, cakes, candy, sugary breakfast cereals), fried foods, fast food, and prepared foods as well as large quantities of soft drinks. They ate in many different places, both regular and fast-food restaurants, in the car, in their room, at a boyfriend's, girlfriend's, or relative's house, and they skipped many meals altogether. The Americans had much less variety in their diets than did the French; although several had turkey and venison, the vast majority stuck to beef, chicken, and pork. There was also less variety in the selection of fruits and vegetables, which consisted primarily of apples, oranges, and bananas, potatoes, corn, and green beans, the vegetables often canned rather than fresh. One telling illustration of the large consumption of prepared foods was that U.S. students tended to specify when a soup, stew, or dessert was homemade. These cultural documents provoked significant discussion regarding cultural differences and students' own eating habits in a way far more complex than was initially expected.

Pedagogical Applications

Such student-generated authentic materials prove effective for several reasons. First of all, they have been produced by peers about their own daily life. The subject matter is familiar and yet provides great diversity of response. The surveys themselves are quite simple, but they stimulate a wide range of activities and discussion topics appropriate to students' ages and abilities. Finally, they provide a well-developed and reassuring context for communication. Exercises based on the surveys promoted communicative activities, cultural observations, and written interchange with the foreign class.

Dividing the class into small groups or pairs to examine a topic offers many occasions for conversation as students read the documents and discuss possible meanings. In larger groups or as a whole, the class can analyze the survey contents statistically, discussing tendencies, exceptions, and expected versus surprising results, always bearing in mind the limitations of the statistical design. Eventually, as the students' proficiency permits, they can prepare a written report on the survey. Here are some examples of communicative activities applicable to such texts:

1. Deciphering the handwritten text or transcribing it into type
2. Checking for spelling errors
3. Listing unknown terms and defining them from context

MONDAY	TUESDAY	WEDNESDAY	THURSDAY	FRIDAY	SATURDAY	SUNDAY
10:00 home muffin glass of milk	10:00 home chocolate Pop-Tart glass of milk	9:45 home chocolate Pop-Tart glass of milk	10:00 home donuts glass of milk		10:30 home donut orange juice	11:00 Erica's house brown sugar Pop-Tart, milk
12:00 home burritos cheese Dr. Pepper	12:30 home salami sandwich Doritos Dr. Pepper	12:00 home patty melt onion rings glass of Coke	11:30 home burritos Coke	12:30 school ham & cheese sandwich chocolate cake chips, milk	12:00 home salami sandwich glass of Coke	2:00 Erica's house sausage pizza Pepsi chips -n- dip
3:00 home chips -n- dip glass of soda			3:00 home grapes		3:30 Erica's house chips -n- dip glass of soda	
7:00 home turkey, corn mashed pota- toes & gravy rolls, milk	6:00 home turkey sandwich chips milk	7:00 home sausage pizza Dr. Pepper	5:30 home pizza rolls glass of Coke	9:30 cheese, pickle hamburger curly fries glass of Coke	6:00 Erica's house chips	6:00 nachos crab Rangoon Dr. Pepper
	9:00 home chocolate chip cookies glass of milk		9:00 home ice cream with chocolate syrup, water		10:30 Erica's house sausage pizza cake, soda	11:00 peanut butter fudge ice cream & hot fudge

Sample Survey Results - American Student (Female age 14)

LUNDI	MARDI	MERCREDI	JEUDI	VENDREDI	SAMEDI	DIMANCHE
7h30 chez moi 1 bol de café 3 pains au lait	9h30 1 bol de café 2 pains au lait	9h 1 bol de café 3 pains au lait	8h30 chez moi 1 bol de café 3 pains au lait	8h30 chez moi 1 bol de café 1 pain au lait	9h chez moi 1 bol de café 2 pains au lait	9h chez moi 1 bol de café 3 pains au lait
13h chez moi 1 salade composée dinde, purée yaourt, orange pain + eau	13h chez ma grand-mère salade + ha-rengs côte de porc choux crêpes, pain	12h30 chez moi 1 sardine à l'huile dinde, pâtes compote pain + eau	12h30 chez moi 1 sardine à l'huile steak pommes de terre yaourt, pain	12h45 chez moi salade + mu-seau vinai-grette carottes jambon yaourt pain + eau	12h30 chez moi salade + thon + tomates côte de porc pâtes banane pain + eau	12h30 chez moi rillettes + pain escalope de dinde pâtes yaourt eau
	17h chez ma tante - crêpes		16h chez moi crêpes		16h chez moi 2 pains au lait	
20h soirée chez des amis 1 salade composée 2 parts quiche rôti de porc froid, chips fromage gâteau (poires) pain + eau	20h chez ma tante soupe poule riz salade de fruits pain + eau	19h chez moi soupe charcuterie escalope de veau haricots verts yaourt pain + eau	19h30 chez moi saucisse choux yaourt pain + eau	20h chez moi potage poisson riz yaourt orange pain + eau	20h30 chez moi potage oeuf sur le plat yaourt pain + eau	20h chez moi avocats garnis (crabe...) fondue (viande cuite dans l'huile) fromage poire Belle-Hélène eau

Sample Survey Results - French Student (Female age 16)

4. Developing categories and categorizing foods

5. Comparing two students' responses or class findings either generally or numerically

6. Filling in missing information (drinks, places, times)

7. Examining how an individual's diet fits into the food pyramid

The list grows as the teacher exploits the particularities of individual responses and addresses student questions.

The teacher need not lecture at all about cultural differences. From a reading and a discussion of survey texts, variations in diet and eating habits become overwhelmingly apparent. In fact, one often has to search consciously for similarities. While no explanations are necessary, much discussion is fostered. At the most basic level, new vocabulary creates an initial obstacle to overcome. Some relatively uncommon food terms were quickly found in a dictionary, but much culinary terminology uses proper names or references not listed in many dictionaries (*friand, carpaccio,* Port Salut, *bigonnaux* [sic]—which was actually *bigourneaux*). The vocabulary and content questions generated from preliminary study included

1. What did the French students drink with their meals? (Many indicated nothing. As U.S. students later found out through correspondence, the French students usually drank water.)

2. Which terms referred to cheeses? (St. Morêt, Kiri, Babibel)

3. What is a *friand? tisane? biscottes? sucette? paëlla? bugnes?*

4. Which dishes are regional or foreign specialties? (*cassoulet, bouillabaisse, rillettes, couscous, paëlla, raviolis*)

5. Which terms are brand names, and do English names refer to the same things? (Kiri, Teisseire, Fanta, Frosties, McChicken, ketchup, Mars)

6. Which terms refer to methods of cooking? (*à la vapeur, parmentier, à la carbonara*)

7. Can French high school students legally drink alcohol? (Not legally under the age of 18, but it is not uncommon for minors to be served beer or wine in social situations)

On the other end, the Americans listed many foods or brand names not available in France—cereals, soft drinks, Pop Tarts—as well as foods for which French students needed an explanation, such as chocolate chip cookie dough, 'Smores, nachos, burritos, and enchiladas. Many U.S. students ate in their cars or in front of the television, while the French generally ate at the table. Another unexpected surprise occurred because the survey began on February 15 just after Valentine's Day. Many U.S. students listed significant amounts of candy, including giant Hershey's Kisses. This led to a discussion among the French students of the holiday and its traditions.

Although many questions that are raised can be answered from context or by the teacher, the best source of information is the corresponding students themselves. Queries can be transmitted and answered via Minitel, ultimately allowing students to produce a written analysis of the survey to be shared with their counterparts. This method of examining cultural differences benefits both classes, as the other group's questions force students to analyze their own behavior.

In addition to topical remarks, other cultural observations unrelated to food occurred. For example, a basic logistical problem arose because the students worked with original documents—the handwriting was difficult to decipher. This allowed students to experience directly a fundamental cultural difference. Rather than having the teacher tell them that handwriting in the L2 culture is different and show samples, students were confronted with the struggle to understand the text. Other remarks concerned paper size, use of graph paper (*papier quadrillé*), and spelling mistakes. By building on the previous list of questions, students formulated others that reflected cultural phenomena more than literal content and dealt with circumstances and preparations of meals, such as

1. Are these foods really served in the school cafeteria? Are there any that are particularly unpopular with students?
2. Do you really eat horsemeat? wild boar? kidneys? brains?
3. Where did you get goose eggs? (One student indicated that she ate goose eggs.)
4. How are various foods cooked? Who cooks at home?
5. Which family members eat together? Why are meals eaten at such regular times?
6. What are the choices for breakfast served at school? How is food served at school? (variety, cafeteria line, seating, etc.)

While it was surmised beforehand that this project would generate usable information, all participants were stunned by the wealth of observations, comparisons, and questions elicited by these materials. The combination of different types of activities, authentic documents, and real communication created an extraordinary learning experience.

Further Applications

Similar surveys can be conducted using a variety of topics applicable to French and U.S. students and would permit students to learn about other aspects of the foreign culture in much the same manner:

1. Each student's class schedule, a typical day
2. Family trees, descriptions of holiday or birthday celebrations
3. Floor plans of students' houses or apartments, a floor plan of the school, a city map, photos
4. Subjects of conversations among friends
5. Exam questions; the table of contents from a textbook, graded homework, study guides, outlines; materials located in the classroom; language or literary texts students are studying
6. Leisure activities, clubs, or sports; itineraries or descriptions of vacation trips
7. Local tourist attractions, museums, monuments, local history
8. Last night's TV listings, what is playing at the movies
9. Prices for various items in stores, newspaper advertisements on a given topic, a shopping list
10. Junk mail

All these topics address practical matters in a student's life, and carefully constructed surveys and their results can build upon students' previous knowledge. A useful framework for conducting a comparative cultural survey involves the following general guidelines:

1. Explain the purpose behind the survey (not scientific, to learn about culture, to prepare authentic documents for the other class)
2. Conduct the survey
3. Exchange the documents by mail or electronic mail
4. Analyze them in various classroom activities
5. Communicate questions and answers about content and general cultural phenomena via Minitel in the language of the culture under study (French students answer questions about their own culture in French and vice versa.)
6. Prepare a report with different groups assigned different areas
7. Exchange the reports
8. Ask for comments and reactions to the report from those surveyed
9. Allow for a follow-up discussion and concluding reactions

Multiple surveys can overlap, and how much use can result from the documents depends, of course, on the topic. Some will prove more interesting and thought-provoking to students than others.

Conclusion

Ideas for a class correspondence activity are limited only by the teacher's imagination, and new ideas may, indeed, grow out of previous exercises. The examination of specific cultural themes through student surveys allows Minitel correspondence to develop from simple chitchat to a real study of language and culture. The opportunities it provides for meaningful exchange and the boost it gives students' motivation to communicate make this an ideal classroom technique. Furthermore, peer-developed materials can stimulate a variety of spoken and written activities, from beginning to advanced study of the language, and can be a great help to teachers in their search for new authentic documents and ways to apply them. A cultural survey combined with a Minitel exchange can provide a catalyst for the development of language proficiency in both students and teachers through real practice. This project can significantly increase cultural awareness both of the target culture and of one's own. What students learn from such an experience will remain with them forever.

Notes

1. Although special Minitel terminals are used in France, from the U.S. the only equipment necessary is a computer (IBM compatible or Macintosh) and a modem. The software is provided free by the Minitel Services Co., and a user is charged for the amount of time he or she is connected to any of the various services. Further information is available from Minitel Services Co., 888 Seventh Ave., 28th Floor, New York, NY 10106, Telephone: 212-399-0080. The Bureau de Coopération Linguistique et Éducative, Consulat Général de France, 540 Bush St., San Francisco, CA 94108, will pair U.S. classes with French classes via Minitel. For teachers of other languages, some Spanish and Italian services are available through Minitel, and the FRANCEMONDE service has subscribers from dozens of nonfrancophone countries as well with whom one can easily communicate.

2. In the fall of 1992, the AATF in conjunction with the French Embassy Cultural Services and Minitel Services Co. offered twelve $300 Minitel Research Award Grants. The purpose of these awards was to allow participating teachers to explore Minitel services and create descriptive *fiches* to be included in an AATF database.

3. I would like to thank the teachers involved, Ramona Shaw, Angel Edgar, Catherine Bouvet, and Dominique Jahan, and their students from Steelville (MO) High School, Salem (MO) High School, the Lycée Professionnel Martin Nadaud in St. Pierre des Corps, and the Lycée Paul-Louis Courier in Tours for their invaluable help in completing this study.

4. The form used one sheet of paper with each side divided horizontally into seven sections to represent each day of the two-week period. Blanks were added for age and sex. This was done merely to facilitate data analysis; students themselves would not need to use a form.

5. Documents themselves could be sent by Minitel, but the volume involved could prove costly, and characteristic problem-solving opportunities such as handwriting and spelling differences would be lost. It was deemed preferable to exchange the survey documents by mail and reserve on-line time for real-time communication about content.

8
Putting Our Proficiency Orientation into Practice through Meaningful Assessment

Donna Clementi
Appleton (WI) High School–West and Concordia Language Villages

Paul Sandrock
Wisconsin Department of Public Instruction

Maintaining Our Vision of Proficiency

When beginning foreign language students are asked why they enrolled in the class, the most common answer is that they want to learn to use the new language; when teachers are asked about their main goal in teaching a foreign language, the most common response is to help students learn to use the language. Keeping the sights of students and teachers on this common goal is the mission of proficiency-oriented instruction. Our number one job as teachers of languages is to continue to develop students' proficiency in speaking, reading, writing, and listening to the language they are learning, always within a cultural context.

How do we maintain this vision? Two key questions will help formulate an answer: (1) how does the curriculum influence instruction and (2) how does assessment reflect the curriculum? *Curriculum* keeps teachers focused and puts our vision or main goal into a framework to guide our day-to-day activity and to make connections from one course to the next. *Assessment* keeps students focused. The common inquiry from students, "Will this be on the test?," is simply a request to be informed about what is truly valued in a course, helping students prioritize areas needing their attention. Omaggio Hadley (1993) has summarized the hypotheses underlying the orientation toward proficiency (see Appendix 8A), and our discussion of assessment will be based on this framework.

Connecting the Pieces

In education, not all goals are equal. This is the underlying principle in a curriculum framework for developing learner goals described by Fortier and Moser (1992) who lay out a taxonomy of educational objectives. These range from (1) *learner goals,* the lofty ideals, what we expect students to know and be able to do as a result of their time in the educational system, to (2) *attributes,* characteristics of learner goals, the more observable descriptors to explain the goals, to (3) *outcomes,* what students can do with what is taught, real-life application, to (4) *enablers,* the knowledge base of the subject area, what a student must know in order to perform the outcome. This format can be useful to differentiate learner goals in various disciplines statewide and to look at goals of individual school districts. Though not designed for any specific discipline, the framework can serve to define program goals in the foreign language context. We can apply this curriculum model, considering how the pieces can fit together, building "bottom up" from the pieces without ever losing sight of the whole.

Structures and vocabulary are a part of the foreign language curriculum; they are the building blocks, the *enablers* that help students reach their ultimate goal of meaningful communication. Structures and vocabulary must be modeled within a real context, however. In first language acquisition, we are able to use language to communicate successfully before we are able to describe the functional aspects of that language. The debate on the order of learning a second language often is a question of the instructional methods used. A "natural approach" will lead to functional use before a student can explain grammatical structures, whereas what one would characterize as more traditional teaching may develop a student's grammar knowledge before that student confidently uses the language. Krashen (1982) makes this distinction in learning mode, where acquisition more closely follows the "subconscious process similar if not identical to the way children develop ability in their first language," and learning is "a conscious process in which the rules of grammar" and their applications are learned (Omaggio Hadley 1984: 46).

There is also a connection to the age of the learner. Young children communicate even though they may use tenses incorrectly and do not know the difference between direct and indirect object pronouns, for example. A key question is how much grammatical terminology a student needs at a given grade level in order to communicate effectively.

As Omaggio Hadley (1984) explores these distinctions, teaching grammatical structures focuses on how to create more accurate communication in students while simultaneously encouraging that communication. Our position here is to see the value of both, since structures are a necessary component of using language. The teaching mode needs to vary with teacher and student characteristics and the purposes of instruction. The important point is to focus on how the pieces must be put in service to the outcomes and broad goals for the foreign language program.

Listening, speaking, reading, writing, and culture skills or proficiencies can be described as *attributes* according to Fortier and Moser's taxonomy by identifying the appropriate degree of proficiency at which we aim to have all our students functioning during the course of the school year. This has been done in the ACTFL (1986) Proficiency Guidelines, which will now help focus the development of national standards for foreign languages. The proficiency guidelines clearly fit a variety of teaching methods; students reach higher levels by becoming increasingly accurate, by being able to apply the language skills in broader contexts (not just in the narrow context in which they were first taught), by being able to give and to incorporate increasingly complete details in the message, and by being able to recombine language elements in new and creative applications. The proficiency guidelines can be used as the basis for developing specific proficiency descriptors for each course offered in a district.

Content and skills are in service to the program *goals*. Program goals include such things as communicating information of personal importance or demonstrating understanding of the ways of another culture. Goals create the reason for giving attention to the content and skills. Goals create the vision of what we really want students to know and be able to do (Diez and Moon 1992).

The important link is the *outcomes,* which connect both the broad goals and their attributes described in level-by-level proficiency criteria with the detailed enablers of language structure and vocabulary. Outcomes are the clear statements of what students will actually do with the language. The outcomes will govern the teacher's choice of assessment tools. They force the teacher to ask continually, "What is important?" and "What is needed for students to communicate effectively at higher and higher levels of proficiency?"

An example will illustrate the interconnectedness of Fortier and Moser's elements. The overarching program *goal* for foreign language students is that they will be able to communicate effectively in their second language. For a level one course, the *attribute* (proficiency descriptor) is that students will be able to speak using short phrases and complete sentences based on memorized elements, showing little recombining ability. The *outcome* to be assessed in several contexts during the year could be that students will describe people or objects in oral and written form. The *enablers* would then be the verb *to be,* forms of adjectives, and a repertoire of adjectives in active vocabulary use. Instruction and assessment are now both focused on giving students the skills, knowledge, and practice necessary to reach the broad program goals. These goals have now been described according to the degree of proficiency appropriate for the cumulative length of time of instruction.

In this example, it must be recalled that the student is still at the ACTFL Novice level. Perfection is not the goal, nor should it be demanded. In assessing this outcome, the teacher will ask, "Was the student able to be understood and to complete the task?" If a student's errors do not impede communication, then he or she can still be assessed positively on the basis of this question.

Making the Assessment Match the Goals

How does a teacher move from a broad curriculum vision to daily instructional decisions? If the focus is only on putting together activities to fill a class period, it is easy to lose sight of the overarching goals. That is why we need a new vision for assessment, to focus on those goals rather than just the pieces. Teachers need to make continuous adjustments to help students move along the proficiency continuum, making assessment the vital link between curriculum and instruction.

The three key planning questions are

1. What do I really want students to know and be able to do? (Curriculum)
2. How will I know when students are there? (Assessment)
3. What can I most effectively do to help students get there? (Instruction)

None of these elements can be an afterthought or a separate decision; rather, they all must influence each other. When we envision the assessment while selecting or creating the curriculum goals, then we have a clearer understanding of what must be done to bring students to that point.

Assessment comes in all types, each type having unique characteristics that need to be matched to desired outcomes. Kraft (1987) has compared assessment types to identify the qualities that will help make the match. Objective tests of the multiple-choice, true/false, fill-in-the-blank, and matching varieties allow teachers to sample the knowledge base of students with maximum efficiency and reliability. The emphasis, however, is on recall, which encourages memorization. The role of such tests needs to be kept in mind so that these are not the only practice or assessment measures used in a course. Oral questions and essay tests allow teachers to catch a glimpse of process as well as content; they are useful in measuring thinking skills, students' use of a particular language structure, and their ability to explain their logic. Direct questions or open-ended questions will also provide a teacher with various insights into how students are thinking. These types of performance assessment gauge the ability of students to translate knowledge and understanding into action. Kraft (1987) cautions that too few samples of performance, vague criteria, poor rating procedures, and poor test conditions can all lead to inaccurate assessment.

Assessment is always a question of matching—the goal of instruction must match the type of assessment and the type of teaching practice must also match the program goals. If a program goal is cultural understanding, then assessment must be provided for that goal. Otherwise, the goal may not directly influence instruction.

An Assessment Framework

Our assessment framework has three components: thematic unit, portfolio snapshot, and summative evaluation. The thematic unit is the tool to reach the proficiency goals by focusing on a cultural topic or a functional goal from the curriculum. Portfolio snapshot is an ongoing scrapbook that shows the strengths and weaknesses of student performance in individual units and also over time.* The summative component finally moves the teacher to evaluate how the skills that were developed in individual thematic units and documented in the portfolio demonstrate the student's progress along the proficiency continuum to reach the broad goals that the local district has identified.

The program goals can no longer be ideals that look good on paper but have no effect on instruction. Goals are real and can be evidenced in the outcomes. Meaningful assessment reflects all elements of the curriculum framework: the building blocks of vocabulary and structure; outcomes; the proficiency descriptors of listening, speaking, reading, writing, and culture skills; and the broad program goals.

The relationship of the assessment components and the program elements is nonlinear, i.e., all parts constantly interact with all the others. Vocabulary and structure are always in tandem, moving from simple to more complex tasks as students' knowledge becomes more sophisticated. The language elements are constantly being put into the purposeful application described in the outcome, which is why assessment must focus on more than vocabulary and grammar.

The development of proficiency is a process, not a product; it is a journey, not a destination. In one sense, "All roads lead to Rome," but the true value of the journey is in how rich the experience is along the way. A student is better at using language by stopping to explore related themes and using language elements in new ways. Students can build more accurate use of language while trying to accomplish meaningful tasks. The portfolio is a diary of these rich experiences on the journey of increasing proficiency.

Putting the Framework into Practice

Matching assessment to program goals does not mean matching one program element to one assessment. Our model provides awareness of the breadth and depth of the planning needed for assessment. It is not intended to be a simple checklist; in fact, assessment often purposefully blends the elements. Evaluation of vocabulary and structure, for example, may blend into a more open-ended summative assessment of the broad goals.

In an activity for portfolio assessment of vocabulary, for example, students may brainstorm the focus topic, drawing as many associations as possible. With the topic in a circle in the middle of the board, students are then challenged to generate as many ideas as possible to explain, define, give examples, compare and contrast, and express opinions on the topic. This phase of the activity can be done as a whole class or in small groups. The assessment activity is for each student, in either oral or written form, to tell as much as possible about the topic, recreating full language from the ideas and single words listed on the topic web. This activity involves some vocabulary recall but focuses most directly on vocabulary usage in a meaningful context. If students truly understand the meaning of the words, usage of the words to recreate complete thoughts is being assessed, not just a translation of vocabulary.

To evaluate student performance, certain questions that identify assessment parameters must be considered:

- Is this a beginning, intermediate, or advanced student?
- Is this a spontaneous or practiced performance?
- Has there been peer/teacher editing, or is the student totally dependent on his/her own knowledge?
- Is assessment based on the amount of different vocabulary used, or should a student simply reach successful completion of the task?
- Is pronunciation of some importance or of a great deal of importance?
- In a written response, what importance will be given to mechanics?
- What elements of structure are important and how important are they?

Putting this into practice for portfolio assessment of proficiency descriptors, a sample student task would be to go to the store and buy items for a picnic. For a level two student, three key criteria could emerge from the questions:

1. Successful completion of the task

2. Extended use of language (variety of vocabulary)

3. Nearly error-free subject–verb agreement for first person

For a level four student, given the same scenario of going to the store, a complication could be added, e.g., the store is out of the type of cheese the student is going to ask for. The student now must use a greater degree of language proficiency to resolve the problem and find out what other types of cheese are available and what the store owner might suggest.

Assessment of the more advanced student will be based on the same questions used for the beginner, but the answers will be different. Structural accuracy and acceptable pronunciation are now significant. There will be more emphasis on extended interaction and the variety of language used. Even at this level there is still room to allow mistakes that do not impede communication; however, in order to move along the proficiency continuum, students should not be continuing to make Novice-level errors. As a student reaches higher levels of proficiency, "acceptable" errors occur in nuances and idiomatic use of the language rather than in basic structures.

It is critical that all language teachers in a school or a school district work together to create criteria for expectations and evaluation for each level. In this way students will not complain to their teacher that last year they were allowed to make mistakes but this year they are penalized for every error. The improvement in accuracy is gradual yet constant.

The study of art is an example of a thematic unit that incorporates proficiency goals. If the focus is to contrast styles of French artists, why teach the unit in French? But if the overall language curriculum goals are intertwined with art content goals, the thematic focus becomes an opportunity to develop more advanced language skills. In the assessment process, students will demonstrate not only their knowledge of the topic (artists), but also demonstrate effective use of appropriate structures and vocabulary in sharing their knowledge. Language becomes a tool as well as a goal; it is now both process and product.

Within this framework, students will select an artist of interest and talk about the artist's style and their favorite painting by the artist. The written assessment could be a summary of the artist's life or a critique of another student's favorite painting. Assessment criteria for the oral presentation would include whether adjective agreement was evident and consistent, whether the historical period was identified and described correctly, and whether suitable vocabulary was used in the response. Smoothness and fluency of pronunciation as well as structural accuracy would be important for upper-level students. In the written element, the structural accuracy and the quality of the information would be evaluated.

While these examples are very task-oriented, we do not mean to imply that this is the only form of assessment or testing taking place. These examples demonstrate clear outcomes. It does not mean that the teacher will not assess the enablers along the way; however, after the "pieces" have been assessed, there is no need to do so again in isolation. Assessment must move to real use of the language.

The area of culture can provide an illustration of a broad goals/summative form of assessment. An anecdotal record of comments made during the year would serve as evidence of movement along the continuum of cultural proficiency. When, for example, beginning-level students stop saying, "That's weird," when hearing of a unique cultural trait or habit and start saying, "That's different," then some progress has occurred. When students are asked to write down questions on what they would like to learn about French-speaking people, the types of questions are a clue to movement toward cultural understanding. Questions like "Is it true that all Frenchmen wear berets?" do not indicate much cultural understanding; however, a question such as "When, where, and how much is wine drunk in France?" indicates that the student may be prepared to view a cultural phenomenon in nonstereotypical terms.

Putting It into Practice: Giving a Grade

An overarching objective of teaching is to help all students work throughout the year toward producing their best work. At the same time, teachers try to help all students move to higher levels of proficiency in all skill categories. The ACTFL (1986) *Proficiency Guidelines* include four strands that define the differences from level to level, and these four strands influence how we develop scoring rubrics for assessment of any skill or outcome. To reach higher ACTFL proficiency levels,

1. *Students demonstrate increasing control and more accurate use of vocabulary and structure.* Spelling and representation of symbols at the Novice–High level in writing "may be partially correct." Intermediate–Low writing still sees "frequent errors in grammar, vocabulary, punctuation, [and] spelling, but writing can be understood by natives used to the writing of non-natives." By the Advanced level, some errors may occur in punctuation or spelling; however, there is evidence of "good control of the morphology and most frequently used syntactic structures." Similarly in speaking, errors become less frequent at higher levels. The student demonstrates no desire to fossilize early errors; accurate use of language is a very real goal. This accuracy is, however, always applied in a personally meaningful context. Accuracy in vocabulary and structure is not an end in itself; the larger goal is real communication.

2. *Students show increasing completeness in producing and receiving communication.* Take as an example an oral or written interview with a soccer star. At early levels of proficiency, students are able to elicit only the gist of the segment. A Novice-level answer would be that the interview is about soccer and the subject of the interview is a good soccer player. Intermediate–Low students could be asked what the soccer player has done to be worth interviewing. An appropriate answer would be that the team has just won a championship and the interview subject scored two goals. At a higher level of proficiency, students would be able to give some details of the player's prior achievements. At the Advanced level, students would be able to draw inferences and describe the player's feelings about his team's winning the championship.

3. *Students demonstrate application in wider contexts.* At the earliest level, students can recall the vocabulary, expressions, and structures only when the context in which they were learned is present. Having learned "What do you want?" in a restaurant setting, the Novice–Mid student would rarely recognize the same question if a teacher used the expression as a student came into the classroom after school. Advanced students would recognize the question out of context.

4. *Students show flexibility to recombine language elements.* Novice-level students do not stray very far from set expressions and responses. Novice–High speaking is described as "relying heavily on learned utterances but occasionally expanding these through simple recombination of their elements." Such students do not yet possess "autonomy of expression." Intermediate students can "create with the language by combining and recombining learned elements, though primarily in a reactive mode." Advanced or Superior students are able to recombine language elements in new and surprising ways and feel comfortable using such recombinations, not only in responding, but also in initiating communication.

If these are the criteria for reaching higher levels of language proficiency, then they must guide our assessment of student progress. The focus on the higher goals of proficiency can be liberating for the teacher. No longer must the teacher feel the urge to cover only a long list of structures and topics; the teacher can truly be a facilitator of student progress along the proficiency continuum. Structures and topics are continuously re-entered during the year as well as from year to year, with increasing expectations of accuracy. In proficiency assessment, the teacher is no longer allowed to hide behind numbers and percentages in giving grades but must trust his or her judgment and make assessments on the basis of several components.

Keeping Focused through Portfolio Assessment

Grading can be easier with the use of portfolios. Not only do teachers get a sense of student progress, but each student is better able to keep informed of progress and know the level at which he or she is functioning. Portfolios can be used to give a sense of a student's proficiency range on any given skill, especially when they contain samples of a wide range of work throughout the term. Examination of this range of performance provides a great deal of information. The ideal is to help each student see movement in two directions: (1) the range of the bracket should shrink, indicating more consistency in performance, and (2) the mean point of the bracket should continually rise to higher levels of proficiency, thus showing progressive improvement. Data collected in the portfolio should provide indicators of this range of performance.

If a portfolio represents only the best efforts of a student, the question of consistency arises. If only certain assessments are identified as being "for the portfolio," pressure is removed from assessment measures that occur in between the portfolio-bound ones. To focus on student progress, however, there must be careful use of the lower end of the portfolio range. Young (1992) has pointed out that if a student's grade represents only a numerical average of all work completed, anxiety becomes a negative factor in some of the assessment activities. If, instead, the grade is generated by an evaluation of student progress, then students have more motivation to do their best, since they are not being penalized for one or two bad grades they may have received during the term.

In addition, if the instructor grades only the last two or three examples of work from a quarter, students may not feel the motivation to do their best during the rest of the term. Students do not yet realize that the process is part of the product. While it may be difficult for the teacher to grade solely on the basis of progress made, some credit should be given for a student's progress. In evaluating progress across proficiency levels, it seems reasonable to give more weight to a student's performance at the end of a grading period rather than averaging all the grades equally.

Throughout this discussion of the proficiency-oriented class, we have raised many difficult questions without easy answers. If a student begins at a low level of performance and makes extreme improvement but is still below the performance of peers, does that student deserve an A for effort? If a student begins at a fairly high level of performance and shows no improvement during the quarter, does that mean that the student does not receive an A? Given the realities of large class sizes and multiple demands on a teacher's day, a proficiency-based assessment framework is admittedly hard to put in place. It is certainly time-consuming. In addition, students have been trained over the years to prepare for knowledge-recall types of assessment. Both teachers and students must learn to use performance-based assessment. It is not an easy task, but the results will more accurately reflect how competently a student uses the language. Only when assessment really measures proficiency can language teachers hope to see the end of a generation of students who say at graduation, "I studied language X for four years and still can't say anything." This is not the end but just the beginning of how we work to put our proficiency orientation into practice.

Note

* For a thorough discussion on portfolios, see the following article by Aleidine Moeller, "Portfolio Assessment: A Showcase for Growth and Learning in the Foreign Language Classroom."

References

American Council on the Teaching of Foreign Languages. 1986. *Proficiency Guidelines*. Yonkers, NY: ACTFL.

Diez, Mary E., and C. Jean Moon. 1992. "What Do We Want Students to Know? . . . and Other Important Questions." *Education Leadership* 49,8: 38–41.

Fortier, John, and Jim Moser. 1992. "Targets and Tasks." Unpublished working paper prepared for the Wisconsin Department of Public Instruction, Bureau of Assessment.

Kraft, Nancy. 1987. "Comparison of Various Types of Assessment." Unpublished chart prepared for the University of Wisconsin–Madison School Evaluation Consortium.

Krashen, Stephen. 1982. *Principles and Practice in Second Language Acquisition*. New York: Pergamon.

Omaggio Hadley, Alice. 1984. "The Proficiency-Oriented Classroom," pp. 43–84 in Theodore V. Higgs, ed., *Teaching for Proficiency, the Organizing Principle*. Lincolnwood, IL: National Textbook.

———. 1993. *Teaching Language in Context*. Boston: Heinle and Heinle.

Young, Dolly J. 1992. "Language Anxiety from the Foreign Language Specialist's Perspective: Interviews with Krashen, Omaggio Hadley, Terrell, and Kardin." *Foreign Language Annals* 25,2: 157–72.

Appendix 8A

Hypotheses Underlying the Proficiency Orientation

Hypothesis 1. Opportunities must be provided for students to practice using language in a range of contexts likely to be encountered in the target culture.

Corollary 1. Students should be encouraged to express their own meaning as early as possible after productive skills have been introduced in the course of instruction.

Corollary 2. Opportunities must be provided for active communicative interaction among students.

Corollary 3. Creative language practice (as opposed to exclusively manipulative or convergent practice) must be encouraged in the proficiency-oriented classroom.

Corollary 4. Authentic language should be used in instruction.

Hypothesis 2. Opportunities should be provided for students to practice carrying out a range of functions (tasks) likely to be necessary in dealing with others in the target culture.

Hypothesis 3. The development of accuracy should be encouraged in proficiency-oriented instruction. As learners produce language, various forms of instruction and evaluative feedback can be useful in facilitating the progression of their skills toward more precise and coherent language use.

Hypothesis 4. Instruction should be responsive to the affective as well as the cognitive needs of students, and their different personalities, preferences, and learning styles should be taken into account.

Hypothesis 5. Cultural understanding must be promoted in various ways so that students are sensitive to other cultures and prepared to live more harmoniously in the target-language community.

9
Portfolio Assessment:
A Showcase for Growth and Learning in the Foreign Language Classroom

Aleidine J. Moeller
University of Nebraska–Lincoln

Keeping track is a matter of reflective review and summarizing, in which there is both discrimination and record of the significant features of a developing experience. . . . It is the heart of intellectual organization and of the disciplined mind.

(Dewey 1938: 87)

Assessment: A Time for Reevaluation?

There has been an explosion of studies and research attempts to find viable alternatives to the practice of assigning students a single letter grade in each subject in school (Jongsma 1989; McLean 1990; Stiggins 1991; Wolf 1988, 1989). It is argued that aspects such as effort, progress, and achievement are often ignored in the single grade and that letter grades indicate neither what students know and can do in a subject area nor the student's strengths and weaknesses. Innovations in curriculum and instruction such as whole language, cooperative learning, and outcome-based education call for a more flexible approach to reporting achievement (O'Neil 1993). Developing abilities should be measured frequently with a multidimensional variety of tasks. Students are encouraged to take risks in the new teaching practices to help them build confidence and encourage creativity. To assign a grade defeats the purpose of the class and can undermine new teaching practices. Because of the limitations that a single grade imposes, several educators have examined the value of using portfolio assessment as an alternative form of evaluation in classrooms (Cambourne and Turbill 1990; Paulson et al. 1991; Valencia 1990; Wolf 1989).

According to educational research, the purpose of an assessment tool is (1) to improve learning and (2) to reveal a range of student skills and concepts that coincide with instructional goals. Arter and Spandel (1992: 36) summarized the desired results and accomplishments for assessments other than letter grades:

1. To go beyond assessing knowledge of facts and include such lifelong skills as ability to learn new information and think independently, and dispositions to learn such as persistence, flexibility, motivation, and self-confidence

2. To portray the process by which students produce work and reveal strategies used for solving problems in addition to the correct solution to the problem

3. To make the assessment congruent with what we consider important outcomes for students (e.g., higher-order thinking skills)

4. To assess within realistic contexts that emulate real-life productions of work

5. To chronicle student development and encourage self-observation of this development

6. To integrate assessment with instruction that encourages active student engagement in learning and student responsibility for and control of learning

Using portfolios of student work for assessment might be one way to accomplish these tasks. Current widespread enthusiasm for assessment through portfolios is a product of unique historical and social conditions.

Historical and Social Contexts of Portfolio Assessment

Alternative forms of assessment—multifariously called authentic assessment (Wiggins 1989), performance assessment (Stiggins and Bridgeford 1985), and dynamic assessment (Cioffi and Carney 1983)—have emerged in the past two decades as a result of (1) calls for rethinking the general purposes, policies, and procedures of standardized testing in the 1980s and (2) a series of conceptual shifts within the field of English language arts. The Reagan years brought a call for accountability that shifted the purpose of testing to comparisons of students' performance (Gomez et al. 1991). According to Linn et al. (1990) this resulted in rising test scores that reflected factors other than increases in achievement and a narrowing of instruction to match the domain of items on a single achievement test (Shepard 1990). Consequently it was recommended that assessment be modified to match classroom experiences more closely. New assessment practices not grounded in standards of the cultural knowledge of one group—white, middle-class, native English speakers—were sought (Haney 1984).

The reform of standardized assessments evolved parallel to a rethinking within the field of English language arts in favor of a more holistic evaluation over discrete analysis (Sulzby 1990; Valencia 1990; White 1984, 1985). Whole-language teaching in reading education, process writing theory and practice, and poststructural literary criticism evolved as products of this development. These developments have underscored the problems in assessment that measure students' learning and achievement from comparisons.

Authentic Assessment: A Demonstration of Learning

The distinguishing features of the new curriculum developments promote (1) demonstrating competence rather than selecting an answer, (2) emphasizing depth over breadth in that projects rather than items are produced, and (3) replacing mechanical scoring by informed judgment (Calfee and Perfumo 1993). Much of whole language in literacy instruction and proficiency-oriented instruction in foreign languages is student-centered in nature, encouraging a demonstration of all skills: reading, writing, listening, speaking (Froese 1991; Omaggio-Hadley 1993). Since students are at the core of these instructional methods, the student should also be an integral part of the assessment procedure. Students should be encouraged to make choices of reading materials and also the methods of assessment used. Process-oriented as well as product-oriented assessment must be considered in the evaluation process. How students develop ideas, organize them, and revise them can give greater insight into gains made in learning than can a single end product. Involving the student in assessment also lends greater insight into the individual student and the progress made. Student-centered diagnostic assessment personalizes the instruction and allows for a gathering of materials over a period of time (Moeller 1993). A variety of holistic assessment techniques that represent real communication situations are offered by whole-language researchers and educators (Froese 1991), and many of these ideas can easily be incorporated into the foreign language classroom (Moeller 1993: 51). Teachers are reclaiming control of the assessment policy requiring students to *demonstrate* what they have learned "bottom up" rather than through standardized or "top down" assessment tools. Alternative assessment represents a paradigm shift, a fundamental change from earlier reliance on standardized testing techniques (Wolf et al. 1991).

Authentic assessment is based on a set of evidence that best shows progress toward goals. The kinds of evidence that reflect desired instructional objectives and communicate what students know therefore consist of a set of artifacts of learning. The portfolio has been successfully used as one way of accomplishing these goals. This assessment tool more closely matches the new curricular goals by revealing what students are doing and the processes they are using to arrive at solutions, as well as documenting student improvement and ability ranges. Through portfolios, teachers and other school professionals have hoped to locate the means to tie together more closely curriculum, instruction, and assessment for all children.

What Is a Portfolio?

Arter and Paulson (1990) have offered a definition that is adapted from one developed by a consortium of educators under the auspices of the Northwest Evaluation Association (NWEA): "a purposeful collection of student work that tells the story of the student's efforts, progress, or achievement in a given area. This collection must include student participation in selection of portfolio content; the guidelines for selection; the criteria for judging merit; and evidence of student self-reflection" (p. 36). This definition supports the goals that assessment be continuous, capture a variety of what students know, involve realistic contexts, communicate to students and others what is valued, portray the processes by which work was accomplished, and be integrated with instruction. Such an assessment tool should allow for input and reflection by both student and teacher and should document the development of student understanding and progress over a period of time.

Students who know clearly what is expected of them can take more responsibility for setting their own academic goals and for assessing their own progress. The assessment process brings about a shift in focus from what teachers "want" of students to what students want for themselves, encouraging a sense of empowerment in students (Lewis 1991). The guiding idea is that portfolios provide an opportunity for richer, more authentic, and more valid assessment of student achievement (Rogers and Stevenson 1988).

Student Involvement

The portfolio movement promises one of the best opportunities for students to learn how to examine their own work and participate in the entire learning process. Students are accustomed to being told what is good and not good in their work. If students are to improve their own judgment about their work, and if their work is to show improvement because of their own struggle with quality, a different use of class and teacher time is required. Students must be helped to make judgments about their work (Graves 1992). Students must constantly write statements in which they evaluate their work throughout the year. Some educators recommend including drafts of written work in order to let students see the development of their writing skills as well as growth over time. The process of writing and growth becomes clear as they examine the evolution of the written work. Readers and writers know more about their own abilities and progress than outsiders do. Thus they can be the prime evaluators of themselves and their work.

To ensure a connection between their lives and their literacy, students put into their portfolios all kinds of work that they see as important to them as learners and that demonstrate they have learned something important. Students are asked to write a short note explaining why they think it belongs in the portfolio. The portfolio thus becomes a history of learning.

Questions arise about the contents to be included in the portfolio. What processes should be used to evaluate the student's work? What standards should be used on the adequacy of student work? How will they be used?

Models of Student Portfolios

Valencia and Calfee (1991) describe three distinctive models in present practice: showcase, documentation, and evaluation. *The showcase portfolio* (Tierney et al. 1991) is a collection of the student's best or favorite work. Most of the entries are selected by the student over time. As a result, the portfolio emerges as a unique portrait of the individual. Self-reflection, self-evaluation, and self-selection take priority over standardization.

The documentation portfolio centers on systematic, continuous evidence of student progress (Goodman et al. 1989). Included are observations, checklists, anecdotal records, interviews, and classroom tests, as well as performance-based assessments. Some of the entries are selected by the teacher, others by the student; some entries are the same for all students, others are different; some are accompanied by student self-reflections, others are judged by external raters. Documentation portfolios do not judge the quality of the activities, but rather provide evidence of documentation.

The *evaluation portfolio* is generally standardized, with considerable direction from the teacher, administrator, or district (Au et al. 1990). Criteria and entries are predetermined for scoring and evaluating performance. A substantial core of required activities dominates the portfolio. Outside personnel may administer some of the assessments to ensure standardization or consistency.

Developing a Portfolio Plan for Student Assessment

The different models involve distinct methods, criteria, purposes, and audiences. Vavrus (1990) has formulated a portfolio plan that serves as a guide for teachers, departments, and school districts in determining which type of portfolio best meets the needs of their students, school, and community. By responding to the following questions posed in this guide, foreign language teachers can create a conceptual framework and formulate the documentation plan:

1. What kinds of assessment are currently used to assess student growth and performance in foreign languages? What do these assessments tell about student learning?
2. What are important aspects of student learning and performance that are not satisfactorily assessed with current practices?
3. What are the buildingwide/districtwide goals that teachers expect students to know and be able to do when they leave?
4. What are the grade-level curricular goals in relation to school-system goals?

Once the conceptual plan has been constructed, the next step is to develop a portfolio documentation plan. Vavrus (1990) suggests building the framework by answering the following questions:

1. What will be the purpose of the portfolio?
2. What documents (work samples, formal and informal tests, observation records, interviews, surveys, journal entries, creative writing) might be included relative to each goal?
3. What are the expectations for students to demonstrate successful growth and learning in relation to each goal?
4. What initial assessment information is presently available for a student's portfolio and how will this information be incorporated into instruction?
5. What kind of student growth documentation for each goal can be generated as part of ongoing instructional activities during the year and how often will these documents be selected for the portfolio? Who will make the selections, the teacher? student? both? Who will prepare reflective captions about what a particular document shows in relation to each goal?

Portfolios in the Foreign Language Classroom

The goal of foreign and second language studies is to prepare students to communicate in natural, real-life situations. "It makes more sense to address the skills necessary, for example, to negotiate a purchase in a drugstore, than to memorize in a vacuum verb paradigms and lists of vocabulary" (Warriner-Burke 1989: 62). Students in a proficiency-oriented curriculum learn to "perform" essential tasks in the target language ranging from simple requests or negotiating a sale to defending a philosophical point of view. Assessment of language in a proficiency-oriented curriculum is necessarily performance-based, "requiring the examinee to apply acquired knowledge to perform designated communication tasks" (Larson and Jones 1984: 116). Assessment should measure a student's ability to perform authentic communication tasks.

Grammar, vocabulary, and pronunciation are also integral parts of the proficiency-oriented classroom, but only insofar as they develop the ability to use the target language for communication (Savignon 1983). Knowledge of linguistic and sociolinguistic rules of usage "should be measured in ways consistent with the proficiency construct underlying that goal. That is to say, *achievement tests should reflect the nature of the proficiency or competence toward which learners are supposed to be advancing*" (Savignon 1983: 246; emphasis added).

According to Carroll (1985: 75), tests should be a "wholesome influence on the program directions and on teaching strategies." They should allow teachers to (1) diagnose students' strengths and weaknesses, (2) determine student progress, (3) assist in evaluating student achievement and proficiency, and (4) evaluate the effectiveness of and suggest improvement for different teaching approaches (Bachman 1990; Shohamy 1991). Assessment in foreign language programs should reflect and support learning and instructional goals. Shohamy (1991) argues for a "portfolio-type" assessment that documents language competence. Samples of evidence of language competence might include writing samples (both draft forms and final forms), interviews, reflective observations, and self-assessments; further evidence might include homework assignments, letters, recorded samples of conversations, skits, and small-group work. It is important to include a variety of language samples "that are more representative of the true language [ability] of the learner" (Shohamy 1991: 165).

Both criterion- and norm-referenced evaluation could be included in the portfolio when they take on new meaning within the context of the other documents found there. For example, if a student's writing samples reflect the same grammatical errors repeatedly, a computerized test on that particular grammar point might be included as evidence of practice and eventually mastery of this grammar point. The emphasis is on including evidence and documents that illustrate growth. Writing samples from levels one to four clearly demonstrate growth in writing skills. It is even more important for the students to analyze their own writing to establish this growth. In other words, a portfolio of writing samples offers the student an opportunity to reflect on learning, thereby engaging in self-reflection. The selection and evaluation of the documents in the portfolio is done *by* the student, not *to* the student. Students learn to value their own work and value themselves as learners. The student is a participant in, rather than the object of, assessment.

Much like the paradigm shift that occurred in the 1970s when the instructional focus in foreign language studies changed from "achievement" to "proficiency," portfolio assessment constitutes a fundamental change from reliance on standardized testing techniques (Wolf et al. 1991) to requiring students to demonstrate what they have learned through production rather than recognition, and through projects rather than items. Reading, writing, speaking, and listening skills are viewed on a continuum requiring ongoing assessment and self-assessment.

The State University of New York conducted an assessment project in foreign languages in order to "develop assessment strategies and instruments that would be compatible with the curricular aims of each department" (Lewis 1991: 35). The organizing principle became the ACTFL–ETS proficiency scale for assessing speaking skills. The university adopted, adapted, or created comparable scales for entry- and exit-level assessments of each of the other skill areas—listening, reading, and writing. The university further sought creative ways to address the issue of literature and culture. After several semesters of work, the result was a substantial shift in departmental thinking away from considering the foreign language major "as a set of courses to be 'covered' or a number of credits to be earned" (Lewis 1991: 37), to one of seeing the learning process as a continuum, one of continual growth. A model of an ascending, expanding, open-ended scale, much like the inverted pyramid, replaced the list of the courses that determined "completion" of the language-learning process. Like Vavrus (1990), Lewis (1991) recommends that each group embarking on alternative assessment plans define its own objectives, identify desired results, and measure its own progress according to local circumstances.

Foreign language teachers and educators have sought to improve the assessment of language learned in the classroom (Larson and Jones 1984; Magnan 1985). One of the greatest classroom discrepancies there are in the foreign language classroom often occurs between the course goals, usually stated in proficiency terms, and the grammar tests that are utilized to measure student achievement (Omaggio-Hadley 1993). If assessment is still grammar-oriented in nature, the effects of curricular innovations are quickly counteracted and the proficiency goals explicitly stated in the course goals are invalidated.

Bartz (1976) pointed out the need to design assessment tools that assess students' ability to communicate authentic meaning. Portfolio assessment offers the foreign language teacher an opportunity to individualize instruction and assessment by measuring growth over time in all skill areas. Audiotapes containing readings and dialogues on the novice level can evolve into spontaneous interviews and role-plays on the intermediate and advanced levels. Journals containing creative writing, letters, summaries, and personal reflection can document development in grammar skills and writing for meaning. Computer E-mail correspondence with another foreign language class or with students in the target culture can be printed and presented as evidence of written communication skills. A variety of video projects created by a group of students such as a skit, a cultural simulation, a play, and commercials can encourage collaboration and foster a sense of community in the classroom.

Shultz and Stark (1992), foreign language teachers at the Illinois Mathematics and Science Academy, use the video as a visual portfolio by which student growth and development in oral proficiency is measured from the beginning of language instruction to its conclusion. Both the teacher and the student are able to assess the students' progress and determine corrective measures to optimize language learning. The imagination is the only limitation to what can be included in a portfolio as evidence of growth toward higher levels of second language proficiency.

As students experience firsthand the development and progress up the proficiency ladder, motivation to continue foreign language study will be greatly enhanced and self-confidence will increase.

Portfolio: An Alliance between Assessment and Instruction

Portfolio assessment is a holistic assessment that allows students to demonstrate what they can do through high-quality, performance-based, meaningful, authentic tasks. Portfolios can also be a powerful force for improving classroom instruction. Authenticity implies a close alignment between assessment and instruction. The shift from teaching discrete grammar skills to an emphasis on processes, application, and reading and writing responses has the potential to generate authentic portfolio entries in context, yielding a fusion between assessment and instruction (Linn et al. 1991). Language learning is conceptualized more as an emerging process than as a set of skills to acquire. The teacher is able to observe students in a broader context: taking risks, developing creative solutions, and learning to evaluate their own work (Paulson et al. 1991). As students become active participants in assessment and develop the ability to become independent, self-directed learners, instruction and assessment are woven together—a key value and rationale for using portfolios.

References

Arter, Judith A., and Peter Paulson. 1990. *Composite Portfolio Work Group Summaries.* Lake Oswego, OR: Northwest Evaluation Assn.

Arter, Judith A., and Vicki Spandel. 1992. "Using Portfolios of Student Work in Instruction and Assessment." *Educational Measurement: Issues and Practice* 11,1: 36–44.

Au, Kathryn H., J. A. Scheu, Alice J. Kawakami, and Patricia A. Herman. 1990. "Assessment and Accountability in the Whole Literacy Curriculum." *The Reading Teacher* 43,8: 574–78.

Bachman, Lyle F. 1990. *Fundamental Considerations in Language Testing.* Oxford, Eng.: Oxford Univ. Press.

Bartz, Walter H. 1976. "Testing Communicative Competency," pp. 52–64 in Renate Schulz, ed., *Teaching for Communication in the Foreign Language Classroom.* Report of the Central States Conference on the Teaching of Foreign Languages. Lincolnwood, IL: National Textbook.

Calfee, Robert C., and Pam Perfumo. 1993. "Student Portfolios: Opportunities for a Revolution in Assessment." *Journal of Reading* 36,7: 532–37.

Cambourne, Brian, and Jan Turbill. 1990. "Assessment in Whole Language Classrooms: Theory into Practice." *Elementary School Journal* 90,3: 337–49.

Carroll, John B. 1985. "Second Language Performance Testing for University and Professional Contexts," pp. 72–78 in P. C. Hauptman, R. LeBlanc, and M. B. Wesche, eds., *Second Language Performance Testing.* Ottawa, Can.: Univ. of Ottawa Press.

Cioffi, Grant, and John J. Carney. 1983. "Dynamic Assessment of Reading Disability." *The Reading Teacher* 36: 764–68.

Dewey, John. 1938. *Experience and Education.* Repr. 1963. New York: Collier, Macmillan.

Froese, Victor. 1991. "Assessment: Form and Function," pp. 283–311 in Victor Froese, ed., *Whole Language Practice and Theory.* Boston: Allyn & Bacon.

Gomez, Mary L., M. Elizabeth Graue, and Marianne N. Bloch. 1991. "Reassessing Portfolio Assessment: Rhetoric and Reality." *Language Arts* 68: 620–28.

Goodman, Kenneth S., Yetta M. Goodman, and W. J. Hood. 1989. *The Whole Language Evaluation Handbook.* Portsmouth, NH: Heinemann.

Graves, Donald H. 1992. "Portfolios: Keep a Good Idea Growing," pp. 1–12 in Donald H. Graves and Bonnie S. Sunstein, eds., *Portfolio Portraits.* Portsmouth, NH: Heinemann.

Haney, Walt. 1984. "Testing Reasoning and Reasoning about Testing." *Review of Educational Research* 54,4: 597–654.

Jongsma, Kathleen. 1989. "Portfolio Assessment." *Reading Teacher* 43,3: 264–65.

Larson, Jerry L., and Randall L. Jones. 1984. "Proficiency Testing for the Other Language Modalities," pp. 113–38 in Theodore V. Higgs, ed., *Teaching for Proficiency, the Organizing Principle.* The ACTFL Foreign Language Education Series, vol. 15. Lincolnwood, IL: National Textbook.

Lewis, Catherine P. 1991. "Assessing the Foreign Language Major at the State University of New York: An Interim Report." *ADFL Bulletin* 21,3: 35–39.

Linn, Robert L., Eva L. Baker, and Stephen B. Dunbar. 1991. "Complex Performance-Based Assessments: Expectations and Validation Criteria." *Educational Researcher* 20,8: 15–21.

Linn, Robert L., M. Elizabeth Graue, and Neill M. Sanders. 1990. "Comparing State and District Test Results to National Norms: The Validity of Claims That 'Everyone Is above Average.'" *Educational Measurement: Issues and Practice* 9,3: 5–14.

Magnan, Sally Sieloff. 1985. "Teaching and Testing Proficiency in Writing: Skills to Transcend the Second-Language Classroom," pp. 109–36 in Alice C. Omaggio, ed., *Proficiency, Curriculum, Articulation: The Ties That Bind.* Report of the Northeast Conference on the Teaching of Foreign Languages. Middlebury, VT: The Northeast Conference.

McLean, Leslie D. 1990. "Time to Replace the Classroom Test with Authentic Measurement." *Alberta Journal of Educational Research* 36,1: 78–84.

Moeller, Aleidine J. 1993. "Whole Language and Foreign Language Proficiency: Natural Approaches to Language Learning," pp. 43–54 in William N. Hatfield, ed., *Visions and Reality in Foreign Language Teaching: Where We Are, Where We Are Going.* Report of the Central States Conference on the Teaching of Foreign Languages. Lincolnwood, IL: National Textbook.

Omaggio Hadley, Alice C. 1993. *Teaching Language in Context.* Boston: Heinle & Heinle.

O'Neil, John. 1993. "The Promise of Portfolios." *ASCD Update* 35,7: 1–5.

Paulson, F. Leon, Pearl R. Paulson, and Carol A. Meyer. 1991. "What Makes a Portfolio a Portfolio?" *Educational Leadership* 48,5: 60–63.

Rogers, Vincent R., and Chris Stevenson. 1988. "How Do We Know What Kids Are Learning in School?" *Educational Leadership* 45,5: 68–75.

Savignon, Sandra J. 1983. *Communicative Competence: Theory and Classroom Practice.* Reading, MA: Addison-Wesley.

Shepard, Lorrie A. 1990. "Inflated Test Score Gains: Is the Problem Old Norms or Teaching the Test?" *Educational Measurement: Issues and Practice* 9,3: 15–22.

Shohamy, Elana. 1991. "Connecting Testing and Learning in the Classroom and in the Program Level," pp. 154–78 in June K. Phillips, ed., *Building Bridges and Making Connections.* Report of the Northeast Conference on the Teaching of Foreign Languages. Middlebury, VT: The Northeast Conference.

Shultz, Willa L., and John Stark. 1992. "Video Portfolio in Foreign Language Oral Proficiency Assessment." Paper presented at ACTFL 1992 Annual Conference, Chicago, November 21.

Stiggins, Richard J. 1991. *Understanding the Meaning of Quality Classroom Assessment: Training Materials for Teachers.* Los Angeles: IOX.

―――, and Nancy J. Bridgeford. 1985. "The Ecology of Classroom Assessment." *Journal of Educational Measurement* 22: 271–86.

Sulzby, Elizabeth. 1990. "Assessment of Emergent Writing and Children's Language While Writing," pp. 83–109 in L. Morrow and J. Smith, eds., *The Role of Assessment in Early Literacy Instruction.* Englewood Cliffs, NJ: Prentice-Hall.

Tierney, Robert J., M. Austin Carter, and L. E. Desai. 1991. *Portfolio Assessment in the Reading-Writing Classroom.* Norwood, MA: Christopherson Gordon.

Valencia, Sheila. 1990. "A Portfolio Approach to Classroom Reading Assessment: The Whys, Whats, and Hows." *The Reading Teacher* 43: 338–40.

Vavrus, Linda. 1990. "Put Portfolios to the Test." *Instructor* 100,1: 48–53.

Warriner-Burke, Helen P. 1989. "The Secondary Program, 9–12," pp. 60–75 in Helen S. Lepke, ed., *Shaping the Future: Challenges and Opportunities.* Report of the Northeast Conference on the Teaching of Foreign Languages. Middlebury, VT: The Northeast Conference.

White, Edward M. 1984. "Holisticism." *College Composition and Communication* 35: 400–409.

————. 1985. *Teaching and Assessing Writing.* San Francisco: Jossey-Bass.

Wiggins, Grant. 1989. "Teaching to the (Authentic) Test." *Educational Leadership* 46,7: 41–47.

Williams, R. L., D. Mosby, and V. Hinson. 1976. "Critical Issues in Achievement Testing of Children from Diverse Educational Backgrounds." Paper presented at the Invitational Conference on Achievement Testing of Disadvantaged and Minority Students for Educational Program Evaluation. Washington, DC: U.S. Office of Education.

Wolf, Dennie P., et al. 1991. "To Use Their Minds Well: Investigating New Forms of Student Assessment," pp. 31–74 in G. Grant, ed., *Review of Research in Education,* vol. 17. Washington, DC: American Educational Research Association.

————. 1988. "Opening Up Assessment." *Educational Leadership* 45,4: 24–29.

————. 1989. "Portfolio Assessment: Sampling Student Work." *Educational Leadership* 47,7: 35–39.

10
Foreign Language Education in the Community College

Richard Kalfus
St. Louis Community College at Meramec

Situated between high schools on one side and universities and colleges on the other, the community college has assumed a unique position in U.S. higher education. Because of escalating costs of higher education and the belief that today's community college student will receive a challenging education in a two-year transfer program, enrollment in our nation's community colleges continues to grow. This is especially true in foreign languages, a traditional component of the first two years of a liberal arts education, where foreign language enrollments have increased over 40 percent in the period between 1986 and 1991 (Berry 1992). A renewed awareness of the importance of foreign language and culture in today's increasingly interdependent world has affected not only enrollment trends in the community college. More importantly, it has made foreign language educators reexamine their teaching methodology, moving them toward a more proficiency-based instruction. With this renewed emphasis in foreign language education come many challenges that must be met by the community college if it wants to sustain the momentum and successfully prepare students for a world where monolingualism may become the exception rather than the rule.

AACC Foreign Language Education Policy Statement

While foreign language education in the community college has much in common with traditional four-year university and college programs, there are many issues special to the community college setting that have to be addressed. Recognizing this, the American Association of Community Colleges (AACC), with a grant from the National Endowment for the Humanities

(NEH), published a Foreign Language Education Policy Statement asserting that foreign language education in the community college is a national priority (AACC 1992). No longer the sole province of transfer students, the study of other languages and cultures should be a part of every community college student's education. AACC's Policy Statement includes fourteen specific recommendations. (See Appendix 10A, *Recommendations to Community College Educators*.) Among the most significant and challenging are the following:

1. Foreign language *proficiency* should be a requirement in most degree programs (i.e., demonstration of a minimum *survival-level* in the four skills).

2. Foreign language study should be placed within the context of an overall policy on the humanities in the liberal or general education program of study.

3. The scope of language study should be expanded to include a broad range of diverse offerings such as language across the curriculum, immersion experiences, and enhanced study-abroad programs.

4. Community colleges should take a leading role in ensuring the continuity of language learning by serving as the link between high schools and four-year institutions.

Recognizing that the distance between a recommendation and its implementation can be a long one to bridge, AACC with NEH funding was able to select fifteen community colleges nationwide (from a pool of eighty-three) to participate in the *Improving Foreign Language Education Project*. These colleges had to demonstrate both the potential and the willingness to implement, in their respective institutions, some components of the fourteen recommendations presented in the AACC Foreign Language Education Policy Statement.

Issues of Common Concern

While the fifteen community colleges had different areas of strength, there were many issues of mutual concern that all wanted resolved. The desire to confront many of these issues became the motivating force behind the written objectives contained in each of the fifteen colleges' Action Plan that was to be implemented during a nine-month period. The areas of concern among the fifteen grant participants are representative of those found in most of the country's community colleges:

1. Many foreign language courses are taught by adjunct faculty who are often hired only shortly before the semester begins; few staff development opportunities are available to them.

2. A sense of isolation exists among many foreign language faculty, who frequently are members of a department with only two or three full-time instructors. Participation in state, regional, and national conferences can help, but special-interest groups are needed within these organizations to focus on the specific issues relating to community college foreign language education. FLES teachers network very well within many foreign language professional groups. A similar supportive environment would be of great benefit to community college faculty.

3. High attrition rates in first-year foreign language courses result in low enrollment in intermediate courses and threaten program continuity. All too frequently third- or fourth-semester foreign language classes with ten or twelve students are canceled (Kalfus 1988).

4. Foreign language departments in community colleges must make a commitment to develop more proficiency-based instructional strategies so that the emphasis is no longer on how many chapters a student covers in a given course, but rather on what he or she can *do* with newly acquired language skills. Course objectives will have to be rewritten to reflect the proficiency movement (Hirsch and Thompson 1992).

5. Communication continues to be poor between the community colleges and four-year institutions. Foreign language faculty, regardless of school level and affiliation, all share one major objective: to promote the foreign language competency of students. They must stop complaining about student deficiencies and stop trying to place blame on the *previous* teacher or *other* school system and begin a joint effort to improve foreign language instruction everywhere.

6. The community college educator has always faced a heterogeneous student body with a wide range of academic ability, from the very gifted student to the developmentally challenged one with very special needs. With increased enrollment in foreign language courses comes the added responsibility to find new delivery systems that better accommodate the diverse needs of the community college student.

Innovative Foreign Language Programs in the Community College

While well aware of the many problems facing foreign language instruction in the community college, we should by no means lose sight of the fact that some of the most innovative, well-conceived, and academically challenging foreign language programs can be found in today's community colleges. They include foreign language certificate programs in international business; immersion and summer/semester study-abroad programs; media-enhanced foreign language programs using the electronic classroom, interactive video, and the state-of-the-art language laboratory; interdisciplinary and foreign-language-across-the-curriculum programs; language proficiency certification programs in which student competency is tested according to the ACTFL *Proficiency Guidelines* (AACC 1992).

Foreign Language Action Plans

Capitalizing on its own strengths and focusing on those areas of greatest concern, each of the fifteen community colleges participating in the AACC Project developed an action plan. Teams composed of two foreign language faculty and at least one administrator with responsibility in curriculum planning worked together in periodic consultation with a mentor, a nationally known foreign language teaching professional. The close collaboration between administrator and foreign language faculty was crucial to the successful implementation of each college's action plan. A creative idea coming from the foreign language educator was continually being evaluated by the participating administrator from a *reality-based* perspective: "Is this feasible on our campus?" Most of the mentors were community college faculty with experience in foreign language teaching, supervision, and curriculum design. They could convincingly validate or reject an element of a team's plan because they already had firsthand experience in a community college environment.

The following is a brief summary of the progress made by foreign language departments in advancing foreign language study while participating in the grant:

Houston Community College System, Houston, Texas, has produced a video demonstrating the proficiency-based approach to foreign language instruction. Exemplary classes of full-time and adjunct foreign language faculty were taped and edited into one video to highlight pair and group activities that allow students to perform real functions in meaningful contexts. The videotape is an ideal faculty development resource for a multicampus community college system with over sixty adjunct instructors. In addition, Houston Community College has established a mentoring system between experienced teachers and new adjunct faculty members.

Greenfield Community College, Greenfield, Massachusetts, must also work with a large number of adjunct faculty. To integrate them better into the foreign language department, several steps were taken: all foreign language classes were assigned to a Monday-Wednesday-Friday schedule to make it easier to arrange voluntary attendance at departmental meetings; the department has been successful in arranging for new faculty to receive payment for attending a required preservice orientation session; a general position paper for adjunct faculty has been developed, outlining departmental objectives and faculty responsibilities. These very efforts on the part of full-time faculty to reach out to adjunct faculty and create a unified spirit within the foreign language department have had a very positive effect on the self-image of adjunct faculty.

Clark State Community College, Springfield, Ohio, has begun addressing the critical issue of articulation between the community college, the area high schools, and four-year institutions. A well-defined needs assessment was conducted that surveyed high school principals, college vice-presidents, and foreign language faculty. Realizing that the college foreign language staff actually did not know *how* foreign languages were being taught in other area colleges and universities, site visits were planned at several institutions to learn firsthand about their curricula and to visit their technology labs.

Shoreline Community College, Seattle, Washington, has begun an effort to encourage foreign language instruction across the curriculum. The college has developed a set of short courses for students not currently enrolled in foreign language classes. These courses have various forms: they are language segments inserted into courses currently taught, one-week units taught in the appropriate languages and added to courses such as Introduction to Business or Asian Studies, and special classes for degree programs such as Spanish for criminal justice majors.

St. Louis Community College, St. Louis, Missouri, working in three specific language groups with representation from adjunct and full-time faculty across a three-campus district, has developed proficiency objectives for first-year Spanish, French, and German. All first-year language students now receive these uniform course objectives, which serve not only as an introduction to the proficiency-based foreign language class, but also as a checklist or inventory to be used throughout the semester to monitor progress in student performance of required language functions.[1] In addition, a self-assessment survey has been designed to assist instructors in evaluating how well they have been able to implement new proficiency objectives. In order to ensure consistency, the survey has been adapted for use in classroom observations (*AACC* 1992).[2]

Where Do We Go from Here?

Regional professional gatherings (such as the Central States Conference, Northeast Conference, PNCFL, SCOLT, and SWCOLT) are ideal for community college faculty to network and discuss how best to improve the quality of foreign language instruction in their home institutions. The Community College Humanities Association, a national organization, is only now beginning to address the very individual needs of foreign language teachers at community colleges. Organizations already involved in issues relating to foreign languages have the opportunity and the obligation to bring more focus to education in the community college. It is important to note that the community college is often the first point of contact between a student and a foreign language; many community college students are the first generation in their families in higher education. The community college represents for so many a crucial transitional stage in their educational and professional development.

There are over fifty community colleges and approximately one hundred fifty full-time foreign language faculty within the Central States Conference region, for example, certainly a large enough and important enough constituency to be considered when planning future conferences. Each of the region's seventeen states might select a community college foreign language representative to assist the conference in determining future issues of mutual concern for community college foreign language faculty. Serving as a liaison between their states' community college foreign language faculty and the regional professional organization, representatives can help establish priority themes to be featured at future community college focus sessions.

Conclusion

There is much to be gained from community college foreign language faculty networking regularly. Confronting issues of common concern at a conference should *not* be viewed merely as an opportunity to complain, but rather as a chance to join forces in problem solving. The number of faculty within our own departments is small when compared to the size of departments of history, English, communications, or mathematics (indeed, many community colleges have only one or two foreign language faculty members). Dynamic, concerned foreign language educators should be able to work together in solving creatively some of the instructional and administrative problems that most dramatically affect community college foreign language teaching. Just as important, community college faculty should take pride in past accomplishments and in the knowledge that they play, and will continue to play, a unique role in increasing foreign language proficiency and cultural understanding among higher education's fastest-growing student population.

Notes

1. For an excellent sample of proficiency-based objectives, see Frank M. Grittner, *A Guide to Curriculum Planning in Foreign Language* (1985), available from the Wisconsin Department of Public Instruction, 125 South Webster Street, P.O. Box 7841, Madison, WI 53707-7841, (608) 266-2188, $21.

2. For a more detailed description of the action plans of all fifteen grant participants, contact Nadya Labib, Assistant Project Director, *Improving Foreign Language Education Project,* AACC, One Dupont Circle NW, Suite 410, Washington, DC 20036, (202) 728-0200.

References

American Association of Community Colleges (AACC). 1992. *Improving Foreign Language Education Grant Newsletter* 1,2.

AACC Board of Directors. 1992. "AACC Foreign Language Education Policy Statement," pp. 5–12 in Diane U. Eisenberg, ed., *The Future of Foreign Language Education at Community, Technical, and Junior Colleges.* AACC Special Reports No. 1. Washington, DC: American Association of Community Colleges National Center for Higher Education.

Berry, David. 1992. "Foreign Language Education at Community Colleges: An Overview," pp. 15–24 in Diane U. Eisenberg, ed., *The Future of Foreign Language Education at Community, Technical, and Junior Colleges.* AACC Special Reports No. 1. Washington, DC: American Association of Community Colleges National Center for Higher Education.

Hirsch, B., and C. Thompson. 1992. "Proficiency Goals and the Teaching of Literature in the Foreign Language Classroom," pp. 61–90 in Diane U. Eisenberg, ed. *The Future of Foreign Language Education at Community, Technical, and Junior Colleges.* AACC Special Reports No. 1. Washington, DC: American Association of Community Colleges National Center for Higher Education.

Kalfus, Richard. 1988. "An Adult Education Foreign Language Program in the Community College: An Innovative Approach." Washington, DC: ERIC Clearinghouse on Languages and Linguistics. [EDSR ED 283 579]

Appendix 10A
Recommendations to Community College Leaders
Making Foreign Language Education a Priority

In order to create a campus climate in which foreign language education can flourish, commitment and support towards implementing the following recommendations must be declared and made public by the faculty and the highest policy and administrative bodies, trustees, presidents, academic deans, and other administrators.

Recommendation 1. The *study* of foreign languages should be highly recommended for all students, including those with academic goals other than a degree program.

Recommendation 2. Foreign language *proficiency* should be a requirement for those degree programs to which it is appropriate. To this end it is recommended that such degree-seeking students be required to demonstrate a minimum of "survival-level" proficiency in the four skill areas of speaking, listening, reading, and writing. ("Survival level" proficiency is the minimum level at which students have the functional ability to ask and answer questions, to speak and write simply about familiar situations in a present time frame, and to negotiate a simple interpersonal transaction.

Recommendation 3. Foreign language programs should be administered and taught by qualified foreign language educators.

Recommendation 4. Each community college, with leadership from its faculty, should develop a comprehensive plan that identifies the purpose and methods of language instruction appropriate to the particular needs of that college's diverse constituency.

Strengthening Foreign Language Education

Foreign language education must be strengthened to engage students beyond the most basic level of language acquisition. Students must also understand and appreciate the cultural context in which other languages are spoken, read, and written.

Recommendation 5. Educational policy concerning language education and the place of other languages in the two-year college curriculum should be framed within the context of an overall policy on the humanities in the liberal or general education program of study; foreign language education should not be considered in isolation, but rather as an integral part of the overall college curriculum.

Recommendation 6. Community colleges should create teaching and learning environments conducive to successful foreign language education by being sensitive to class size, faculty teaching loads, the attainment of appropriate training for all faculty, and an appropriate balance between full-time and part-time faculty.

Recommendation 7. Foreign language instruction should broaden, and not compete with, required humanities courses. Historical, literary, philosophical, cultural, and other works in the arts and humanities should be infused into all language courses and programs.

Recommendation 8. Community colleges should examine ways in which new technologies, used in conjunction with qualified foreign language educators, can enhance language instruction.

Recommendation 9. In addition to basic and intermediate level foreign language courses, community colleges should expand the scope of language study to include a broad range of diverse offerings such as languages-across-the-curriculum programs; immersion experiences and enhanced study abroad programs; paired humanities/foreign language courses; cross-cultural institutes, workshops, and conferences.

Recommendation 10. Community colleges should enrich their foreign language programs by reaching out to their local community of native speakers, including those in professions, business, and government agencies.

Strengthening Faculty Development

To encourage and assist language teachers in enhancing their scholarship, refining their teaching skills, and continuing in the profession, the following recommendations are offered:

Recommendation 11. Faculty development resources and external funds should be made available to help language faculty to:

• further their knowledge and proficiency
• improve their teaching skills
• design new programs
• develop competency in oral proficiency assessment
• learn new applications of technology

Recommendation 12. Full-time faculty and, where possible, part-time faculty, should be encouraged, supported, and rewarded for active involvement in scholarship and the activities of professional organizations which focus on the quality and improvement of language instruction.

Improving Articulation

Continuity in language learning is essential to effective foreign language education; it must take place throughout the educational process. Community colleges, serving as the link between high schools and four-year institutions, are well-positioned to address problems that now impede articulation.

Recommendation 13. Community colleges should take a leadership role in their service areas to build an alliance of elementary, secondary, two- and four-year colleges, graduate schools, and other appropriate local bodies to address the full spectrum of articulation and continuity issues in language education.

Recommendation 14. Community colleges should initiate communication with four-year colleges and graduate schools in their service areas regarding teacher education, so that these institutions can come to understand the instructional needs of the diverse two-year student body and develop better prepared teachers to meet those needs.

These recommendations, developed to make foreign language education a priority at community colleges nationwide, should be circulated widely to boards of trustees, college administrators, legislative officials, and college faculty, as well as to public and private press and other media.

Suggested Readings

Defining the Profession

Celis, William III. "The Fight over National Standards." *New York Times,* Aug. 1, 1993, sec. 4A.

This article addresses the national curriculum controversy associated with the development of national standards in various disciplines, including foreign languages.

Early, Penelope M. "The Teacher Education Agenda: Policies, Policy Arenas, and Implications for the Profession," pp. 7–22 in Gail Guntermann, ed., *Developing Language Teachers for a Changing World.* The ACTFL Foreign Language Education Series, vol. 23. Lincolnwood, IL: National Textbook, 1993.

The author discusses the impact points for reforming teacher education, the effect of standards on teacher education, and the role of teacher education within the broader education reform movement.

LaBouve, Robert W. "Proficiency as a Change Element in Curricula for World Languages in Elementary and Secondary Schools," pp. 31–51 in June K. Phillips, ed., *Reflecting on Proficiency from the Classroom Perspective.* Northeast Conference Reports. Lincolnwood, IL: National Textbook, 1993.

The work provides an overview of the evolution of performance standards and compares efforts in Indiana, New York, North Carolina, and Texas to develop standards in foreign language education.

Swaffar, Janet. "Using Foreign Languages to Learn: Rethinking the College Foreign Language Curriculum," pp. 55–86 in June K. Phillips, ed., *Reflecting on Proficiency from the Classroom Perspective.* Northeast Conference Reports. Lincolnwood, IL: National Textbook, 1993.

This article calls for the development of coherent foreign language programs in higher education and explores the use of performance standards in colleges and universities.

Addressing Diversity

Banks, James, and Cherry A. McGee-Banks, eds. *Multicultural Education: Issues and Perspectives*. Boston: Allyn and Bacon, 1989.

A collection of readable articles on diverse aspects of multicultural education. All the articles are based on the need for U.S. education to celebrate diversity rather than ignore it. Teachers will find the practical examples useful, although the articles do not deal specifically with foreign languages. It is a good background reader for anyone interested in intercultural relations within the general topic of schooling.

Bartel, Nettie R., and S. Kenneth Thurman. "Medical Treatment and Educational Problems in Children." *Phi Delta Kappan* 74,1 (1992): 57–60.

This article provides an overview of childhood diseases (usually due to inadequate prenatal care) and the effect they can have on children's future learning.

Brophy, Jere. "Synthesis of Research on Strategies for Motivating Students to Learn." *Educational Leadership* 45,2 (1987): 40–48.

One of the reasons students are at risk is that they are unmotivated. This reading is a comprehensive synthesis of research on motivation. Its suggestions are excellent for all students.

Burgess, Donna M., and Ann P. Streissguth. "Fetal Alcohol Syndrome and Fetal Alcohol Effects: Principles for Educators." *Phi Delta Kappan* 74,1 (1992): 24–29.

The authors describe in detail the effects on children when exposed to alcohol as fetuses.

Carnegie Foundation for the Advancement of Teaching. *The Imperiled Generation*. New York: Carnegie Foundation for the Advancement of Teaching, 1988.

This report documents the current developments threatening today's youth. The document provides statistics.

Frymier, Jack. "Children Who Hurt, Children Who Fail." *Phi Delta Kappan* 73,3 (1992): 257–59.

Frymier makes a strong and poignant case for the sad conditions that affect children in the 1990s. He provides statistics that point out that we must take action to correct the trend.

Griffith, Dan R. "Prenatal Exposure to Cocaine and Other Drugs: Developmental and Educational Prognoses." *Phi Delta Kappan* 74,1 (1992): 30–34.

The article provides a description of the damage illegal drugs cause to unborn children. This article is especially current, since a new generation of children exposed to crack cocaine have reached the elementary school.

Hale-Benson, Janice. *Black Children: Their Roots, Culture, and Learning Styles*, rev. ed. Baltimore: Johns Hopkins University Press, 1988.

This is an interesting and readable study of the ways in which African-American children are affected in school learning by their home environment and upbringing. For those particularly interested in FLES, the author's emphasis on language arts will be informative. This is a very important resource for those interested in learning styles and achievement.

Hamby, John V. "How to Get an 'A' on Your Dropout Prevention Report Card." *Educational Leadership* 44,6 (1987): 60–61.

This is a must-read article for all teachers. It provides solid suggestions on how to be an effective teacher for all students.

Hilliard, Asa G., Lucretia Payton-Stewart, and Larry Obadele Williams, eds. *Infusion of African and African-American Content in the School Curriculum: Proceedings of the First National Conference.* Detroit: Aaron Press, 1990.

An important work for those seeking ways to include cultural content and perspectives relating to African-American students, this proceedings book is an excellent resource. It builds a case for the deliberate inclusion in the general curriculum of the content stated in the title, and it speaks to the importance of nurturing African-American students' self-concept. School administrators, supervisors, and classroom teachers should find this book interesting reading.

Lloyd, R. Grann, ed. "The Plight of Black Males in America: The Agony and the Ecstasy." *The Negro Educational Review* 43,1–2 (January-April 1992).

A collection of papers dealing with the plight of the African-American male in today's society presents important perspectives on how to meet the challenge. Each of the eight authors affirms the transforming value of education as a liberating force. The publication should be useful both for those who are interested in understanding the issues and for those seeking decisive action to help resolve them.

Miere, Kenneth J., Joseph Stewart, Jr., and Robert E. England. *Race, Class and Education: The Politics of Second-Generation Discrimination.* Madison: Univ. of Wisconsin Press, 1989.

An excellent research-based analysis of issues dealing with educational access of African-Americans in 174 school districts throughout the United States. The authors argue that academic grouping and disciplinary processes have resulted in a separation of African-American and European-American students in the schools, with the education of African-American students being inferior to that of European-American students. The book presents an excellent analysis of the issues.

National Center for Health Statistics. *Calculations by the Children's Defense Fund.* Washington, DC: U.S. Department of Health and Human Services, 1989.

This document provides statistics on the status of the health and well-being of today's children.

Needleman, Herbert. "Childhood Exposure to Lead: A Common Cause of School Failure." *Phi Delta Kappan* 74,1 (1992): 35–37.

Many children of all socioeconomic classes have been exposed unknow-ingly to lead paint. This article offers a strong description of the problem and points to what teachers can do for children suffering from this condition.

Schlesinger, Arthur M., Jr. *The Disuniting of America: Reflections on a Multicultural Society.* New York: W.W. Norton, 1992.

This book convincingly argues against the "melting pot" theory that for decades was used to explain the composition of our society. Instead Schlesinger offers a dismal picture of the path we are following.

Sleeter, Christine, and Carl Grant. *Making Choices for Multicultural Education: Five Approaches to Race, Class and Gender.* New York: Macmillan, 1994.

This is a noteworthy discussion of how schools could work to meet the needs of a diversified student population. The authors include a synthesis of research and theory underlying five approaches to multicultural educa-tion and show how these approaches can be applied to various forms of diversity.

Steele, Claude M. "Race and the Schooling of Black Americans." *Atlantic Monthly* 269,4 (1992): 68–78.

This is a must-read article for any educators who need to understand issues relating to race and school achievement, particularly African-Ameri-can students. African-American students are taught from their initial formal schooling through graduate studies that they are not expected to achieve in school. Students who accept this characterization unfortunately tend to drop out of school, fail to achieve their potential in school, and often do not see themselves as winners. Written by a social psychologist, this article should be required reading for all educators.

Treisman, Uri. "Academic Perestroika: Teaching, Learning, and the Faculty's Role in Turbulent Times." Unpublished manuscript. (Available from the author, see Chapter 2, note 3.)

Building on his work over the past decade, the author sets forth a novel approach by which African-American and Hispanic students are educated. Examples are drawn from math and science instruction, but clear applica-tions to other disciplines can be seen. The assumption is made that culture (e.g., social interactions between ethnic group members) can serve as a basis for formal learning. A very worthwhile document with a college student orientation.

Trueba, Henry. *Raising Silent Voices: Educating the Linguistic Minorities for the 21st Century*. New York: Newbury House, 1989.

This book represents an assessment of the situation of linguistic minorities and some of the problems they experience in the school system. There are suggestions and recommendations for designing educational programs more appropriate to linguistic minorities.

Re-Viewing the Curriculum

Baker, Colin. *Foundations of Bilingual Education and Bilingualism*. Clevedon, Eng.: Multilingual Matters, 1993.

This article is an in-depth treatment of bilingualism from a psychological and sociological perspective, with extensive discussion of sociolinguistic, psycholinguistic, pedagogical, and political issues related to bilingualism and bilingual education.

Banks, James. *Multiethnic Education: Theory and Practice*. Boston: Allyn and Bacon, 1981.

A discussion of the philosophical and definitional issues related to pluralistic education, the book includes suggestions for designing and implementing effective teaching strategies that reflect ethnic diversity. There are also guidelines for multiethnic programs and practices.

Dow, James, ed. *Language and Ethnicity. Focusschrift in Honor of Joshua A. Fishman*. Amsterdam, Neth.: John Benjamins, 1991.

This collection of essays provides an international perspective on recent research devoted to the issue of language and ethnicity. Several of the articles focus on the language of ethnic minorities in the United States.

Fishman, Joshua A. *Language and Ethnicity in Minority Sociolinguistic Perspective*. Clevedon, Eng.: Multilingual Matters, 1989.

Various issues of language, ethnicity, nationalism, and cultural heterogeneity are raised in this collection of essays by Fishman. The work highlights ethnocultural and ethnolinguistic concerns in social theory and underscores the pluralistic nature of society.

Grant, Carl, ed. *Research and Multicultural Education: From the Margins to the Mainstream*. London, Eng.: Falmer, 1992.

These essays stress the importance of research in multicultural education and contribute to the research base in this area. There is some discussion of multicultural education policy as it pertains to teacher education.

Hirsch, Bette G. "A Proficiency-Based French Conversation Course." *French Review* 59,2 (1985): 210–18.

This article describes an interesting proposal for a proficiency-based conversation class with mixed-level students. Students are made responsible for their own progress by pledging to follow a "goal contract" that is based on functions related to the ACTFL proficiency scale.

Kramsch, Claire. "Literary Texts in the Classroom: A Discourse." *Modern Language Journal* 69,1 (1985): 356–66.

This article goes beyond the use of literary texts as informational input in language teaching. It illustrates techniques for "interpreting and understanding the symbolic nature of a literary text at its cultural, social, and historical dimension." Excellent bibliography.

Nunan, David. "Hidden Agendas: The Role of the Learner in Programme Implementation," pp. 176–86 in R. K. Johnson, ed., *The Second Language Curriculum*. Cambridge, Eng.: Cambridge Univ. Press, 1989.

This chapter reports research on learners' perceptions of the learning process and brings to light the mismatches between goals of the official curriculum and what learners actually learn. It includes a discussion of the implications of these findings for teaching and for implementation of a communicative language curriculum.

Padilla, Amado, Halford Fairchild, and Concepción Valadez, eds. *Foreign Language Education: Issues and Strategies*. Newbury Park, CA: Sage, 1990.

This collection of articles deals with various issues related to foreign language education, including political, historical, demographic, social, and instructional perspectives as well as immersion programs in foreign language education.

Pattison, P. *Developing Communication Skills: A Practical Handbook for Language Teachers with Examples in English, French, and German*. Cambridge, Eng.: Cambridge Univ. Press, 1987.

The section "Developing Communication Skills" (pp. 5–24) contains an excellent summary of the tenets and rationale of communicative language teaching. The rest of the book is devoted to dozens of activities, and section 4.1 gives useful inventory of communication strategies.

Paulston, Christina Bratt. *Sociolinguistic Perspectives on Bilingual Education*. Clevedon, Eng.: Multilingual Matters, 1992.

Theories and research in bilingual education are the focus of this collection of articles. All underscore the importance of the social relationship of linguistic groups in interpreting bilingual education.

Phillips, Elaine M. "Anxiety and Oral Competence: Classroom Dilemma." *French Review* 65,1 (1991): 1–14.

This article skillfully disentangles the issues of language anxiety and second language achievement, and it offers general strategies for coping with student anxiety ("rational emotive therapy," encouraging realistic expectations in language learning). Thorough bibliography.

Reynolds, Allan, ed. *Bilingualism, Multiculturalism, and Second Language Learning*. Hillsdale, NJ: Erlbaum, 1991.

Articles dealing with various topics related to second language learning in a pluralistic society have been collected for this work. Subjects range from issues of assimilation and multiculturalism to language planning. There is also some discussion of bilingualism.

Richards, Jack, and David Nunan. *Second Language Teacher Eduction*. Cambridge, Eng.: Cambridge Univ. Press, 1990.

The authors analyze issues, trends, approaches, and practices in second language teacher education with suggestions and ideas for program design.

Wallace, Michael. *Training Foreign Language Teachers: A Reflective Approach*. Cambridge, Eng.: Cambridge Univ. Press, 1991.

Various issues that pertain to the professional development and competence of foreign language teachers are presented here, including the framework of a coherent approach to foreign language teacher education. The author lists activities and makes practical suggestions for foreign language teacher education and supervision.

Encountering Other Cultures

AATF National Bulletin.

Starting with volume 16, this publication provides regular updates on Minitel services and the activities of the AATF Telematics Commission.

Abrate, Jayne. "Cuisiner avec Minitel: Minitel Services Award Project Report." *AATF National Bulletin* 19,2 (1993): 20–21.

The author reports on a project examining food-related Minitel services and offers guidelines for conducting a comprehensive Minitel search. Suggestions for pedagogical uses and a sample *fiche d'activité* are provided.

Behal-Thomsen, Heinke, Angelika Lundquist-Mog, and Paul Mog. *Typisch deutsch? Arbeitsbuch zu Aspekten deutscher Mentalität*. Munich, Ger.: Langenscheidt, 1993.

This excellent student workbook applies Paul Mog's study, "Die Deutschen in ihrer Welt," to classroom projects. Authentic reading materials and pictures focus on the study of "German mentality," and the suggested activities challenge preconceived stereotypes. The book is a cultural reader that contrasts German and American ways of thinking. Students in advanced high school courses and at the college level will benefit most from this book.

Bowles, Paul. *The Sheltering Sky*. New York: Vintage, 1990.

Paul Bowles explores ways in which Americans approach a new culture and how they are discomfited by their own incomprehension. This novel, first copyrighted in 1949, is great reading for the foreign language teacher interested in the subtle affective and cognitive dimensions of understanding a strange culture.

Bredella, Lothar, and Dietmar Haack, eds. *Perceptions and Misperceptions: The United States and Germany. Studies in Intercultural Understanding.* Tübingen, Ger.: Narr, 1988.

This book is a report on a conference held in Gießen, Germany, in 1986. Thirteen articles by German and American scholars address the question of how intercultural understanding is possible. The theoretical readings approach the topic from philosophical, linguistic, and literary perspectives.

Byram, Michael. *Cultural Studies in Foreign Language Education.* Clevedon, Eng.: Multilingual Matters, 1989.

This work represents a theoretical and practical investigation of the educational value of cultural studies in the foreign language teaching curriculum. There is considerable discussion of methodology, techniques, and assessment of the teaching of cultural studies.

Challe, Odile. "Le Minitel: La Télématique à la française." *French Review* 62,5 (1989): 843–56.

This historical outline of the development of Minitel also describes its organization and the Minitel phenomenon in France. This is an excellent introduction to what Minitel is and how it works.

Challe, Odile. "Les Spécificités d'un média moderne: La Télématique." *AATF National Bulletin* 16,3 (1991): 11–14.

The author analyzes the communications and pedagogical implications of recent technological developments on the study of foreign languages, using Minitel as an example for French.

Edelhoff, Christoph, and Eckart Liebau, eds. *Über die Grenze. Praktisches Lernen im fremdsprachlichen Unterricht.* Weinheim, Ger.: Beltz, 1988.

Sixteen articles describe classroom projects designed by teachers in Germany. The reader gets valuable and practical ideas from the activities in literature, theater, play, and school partnership projects.

Frisch, Max. *Homo Faber*. Frankfurt am Main, Ger.: Suhrkamp, 1969.

In this classical novel first copyrighted in 1957, the Swiss author describes the difficult process of accepting other people and other cultures. Faber, the protagonist, travels to other countries and sees his view of the world challenged by the customs and behavior of the people he meets. To a certain extent, he is trying to discover his own identity through a renewed understanding of others.

Gray, Eugene. "Technology and the Teaching of French Civilization: La Télématique." *French Review* 61,3 (1988): 504–8.

This brief introduction to Minitel in the context of French industrial and business achievements provides a short description of Minitel functions and services.

Hunfeld, Hans. *Geschichten vom deutschen Amerika*. Bochum, Ger.: Kamp, 1984.

These stories are entertaining and full of insights into the way Germans perceive Americans. Too much information about America or information that cannot be processed may distort a perception of American culture.

Hunfeld, Hans. *Literatur als Sprachlehre. Ansätze eines hermeneutisch orientierten Fremdsprachenunterrichts*. Munich, Ger.: Langenscheidt, 1990.

Culture is primarily a communicative phenomenon. Semioticians contend that understanding other cultures means understanding what people say. Understanding and interpreting literature follows essentially the same hermeneutic process. The author describes approaches to understanding a culture by reading literary texts in the classroom.

Johnson, Mark, and George Lakoff. *Metaphors We Live By*. Chicago: Univ. of Chicago Press, 1980.

In their linguistic and philosophical study of a wealth of everyday metaphors in the English language, the authors construct a powerful study of how culture-bound images influence our ways of thinking. The interested foreign language teacher will enjoy the concrete examples and gain a sharpened sense of why the teaching of foreign languages must go far beyond linguistic structures and dictionary meanings.

La Lettre de Télétel.

This newsletter offers information on improvements, commercial prospects, equipment, and other matters for users and business customers in France.

Marchand, Marie. *La Grande Aventure du Minitel*. Paris, Fr.: Larousse, 1987.

This book outlines the technical creation and development of Minitel and examines the sociological changes it has created.

Mayer, Joel. "Minitel in the High School Classroom: From Illiteracy to Fanaticism in Six Short Months." *AATF National Bulletin* 16,2 (1990): 13.

The author describes his personal experiences in learning to use Minitel and incorporating it into the classroom. The article includes practical logistical suggestions for high school classes.

Minitel: la B.D. du prof.

This newly created newsletter offers helpful suggestions and examples for using Minitel services in the classroom. The information in the first three issues includes sample activities and Minitel screens as well as technical information.

Minitel Télématique: Livret Pédagogique. San Francisco: Consulat de France.

This short booklet presents information on using several Minitel services in the classroom in the form of *fiches de service* describing cost, function, operation, and contents. It also includes a description of the EDUTEL service of the French Ministry of Education.

Shelley, Janine Onffroy. "SNCF: A Document to Acquaint Students with the SNCF prepared by using the Minitel." *AATF National Bulletin* 17,2 (1991): 9–12.

This article offers concrete examples of exercises on time, geography, and taking the train, giving sample screens from the SNCF Minitel Service. Screens were prepared using a Macintosh computer.

Steg, Adam, and Townsend W. Bowling. "Minitel Technical Guide." *AATF National Bulletin* 16,4 (1991): 9–12.

The authors give a systematic description of Minitel and how to access it as well as a brief glossary of terminology.

Measuring Proficiency

Arter, Judith A., and Vicki Spandel. "Using Portfolios of Student Work in Instruction and Assessment." *Educational Measurement: Issues and Practice* 11,1 (1992): 36–44.

This is a training module intended to clarify the notion of portfolio assessment and help users design such assessments in a thoughtful manner. Rationale for assessment alternatives as well as a discussion of portfolio definitions, characteristics, pitfalls, and design considerations are included.

Calfee, Robert C., and Pam Perfumo. "Student Portfolios: Opportunities for a Revolution in Assessment." *Journal of Reading* 36,7 (1993): 532–37.

This is a survey of portfolio practices that raises concerns about this movement and offers suggestions on how it can realize its promises.

DeMado, John. *From Mastery to Proficiency: Shifting the Paradigm.* Washington, CT: Sisyphus, 1993.

The author challenges teachers to teach and test for real communication in the second language.

Graves, Donald L., and Bonnie S. Sunstein, eds. *Portfolio Portraits.* Portsmouth, NH: Heinemann, 1992.

The first section of *Portfolio Portraits* illustrates classes in which portfolios are kept—first grade, fifth grade, eighth grade, sophomore year of college, and graduate course for teachers. The chapters describe how portfolios can link theory and practice for students and teachers. The second section takes a look at the larger issues related to portfolios: self-evaluation, classroom climate, testing, and performance assessment. The third section offers four portraits of very different people who keep portfolios: a school superintendent, a college senior, and two second graders.

Herman, Joan L., Pamela R. Aschbacher, and Lynn Winters. *A Practical Guide to Alternative Assessment.* Alexandria, VA: Association for Supervision and Curriculum Development, 1992.

The authors examine alternative assessment and list strengths, weaknesses, and appropriate uses for a variety of assessment tools. They also discuss how to begin designing alternative assessments.

Newmann, Fred. "Linking Restructuring to Authentic Student Achievement." *Phi Delta Kappan* 72,6 (1991): 458–63.

The author states that the restructuring of U.S. schools will not positively affect student success unless planners keep desired outcomes for student learning in mind.

Shohamy, Elana. *The Power of Tests: The Impact of Language Tests on Teaching and Learning.* Washington, DC: The National Foreign Language Center, 1993.

The author reports on three studies of the use of language tests and their impact on students, teachers, and policymakers. She answers the question, "Can the introduction of tests cause real improvement in learning and teaching?" Study showed that instruction came to resemble tests, which underscores the need for diagnostic feedback from tests to influence instruction.

Simmons, Warren, and Lauren Resnick. "Assessment as the Catalyst of School Reform." *Educational Leadership* 50,5 (1993): 11–15.

The authors view performance standards as a way for schools to examine how effectively they are delivering instruction. Through the establishment of meaningful assessments, all students will have equal opportunity to reach world-class standards.

Wiggins, Grant. "A True Test: Toward More Authentic and Equitable Assessment." *Phi Delta Kappan* 70,9 (1989): 703–13.

The author encourages educators to examine the purpose and authenticity of any student assessment. He stresses the need for matching the form of assessment with clear, meaningful goals in order to inform instruction. He argues that a true test requires the performance of exemplary tasks and involves students in the actual challenges and standards of the discipline or workplace. The author challenges the bell-curve approach to testing, urging collaborative assessment that reveals students' reasoning.

Wiggins, Grant. "Creating Tests Worth Taking." *Educational Leadership* 49,8 (1992): 26–33.

Wiggins details criteria to assist reformers in developing valid performance assessments that are meaningful and engaging to students. The author gives specific guidelines for choosing what to test, contextualizing the task in a meaningful way, challenging students to use higher-order thinking, establishing scoring criteria, and implementing this new type of assessment in order to support school reform.

Wolf, Dennie, Janet Bixby, John Glenn III, and Howard Gardner. "To Use Their Minds Well: Investigating New Forms of Student Assessment." *Review of Research in Education* 17 (1991): 31–74.

This thorough article discusses the transition from a testing culture to an assessment culture. The authors describe several approaches to assessment that seem promising as productive means of not only monitoring but also promoting student learning, including developmental assessments, performance tasks, exhibitions, and portfolio-like processes. Especially valuable is the history and rationale of testing. Several models and examples are provided to illustrate models of assessment, illuminate the capacities of a wide range of students, and offer useful information about learning and teaching.

Serving the Wider Community

Borchardt, Frank L. "Press Any Key to Continue: Technology and Fantasy for the Rest of the 90s." *CALICO Journal* 8,4 (1991): 17–24.

Computers will not replace teachers, but teachers who use computers will replace teachers who don't.

New Directions for Community Colleges 18,2 (1990).

Designed to assist community colleges in developing effective international education programs, this monograph contains eleven essays that discuss ways to develop successful programs.

Harper, Jane, and Madeleine Lively. "Conversation Classes: Activities and Materials That Encourage Participation." *Foreign Language Annals* 20,4 (1987): 337–44.

The authors describe innovative materials and activities used by Tarrant County (Texas) Junior College in its conversation classes for high school and college students. The article also includes a discussion of career-ladder credit conversation courses for foreign language teachers.

Horwitz, E., and D. Young, eds. *Language and Anxiety.* Englewood Cliffs, NJ: Prentice-Hall, 1991.

This study is of particular interest to community college educators, who often teach first-time foreign language students. Many practical suggestions are offered to reduce anxiety and raise students' written and oral performance.

Knerr, Jennifer L. "Teaching the Working Adult and Retiree: Considerations for the Nontraditional Classroom," pp. 92–109 in William N. Hatfield, ed., *Creative Approaches in Foreign Language Teaching.* Report of the Central States Conference on the Teaching of Foreign Languages. Lincolnwood, IL: National Textbook, 1992.

The author offers practical techniques to deal with problems such as hearing, vision, memory, motivation, purpose, age, and fatigue, among others, that are often found in the advanced-age student.

Tamarkin, Toby. "Intensive Language Programs: Two Models for the Community College." *Hispania* 71,1 (1988): 177–79.

The article describes adoption of an intensive (Spanish) language program to suit the needs of two-year community colleges, resulting in student enthusiasm, increased enrollment, and more comprehensive coverage of material.

Central States Conference Proceedings

Published annually in conjunction with the
Central States Conference on the Teaching of Foreign Languages

For further information or a current catalog, write:
National Textbook Company
a division of *NTC Publishing Group*
4255 West Touhy Avenue
Lincolnwood, Illinois 60646-1975 U.S.A.